Edited by Neil Spiller
and Aleksandra Wagner

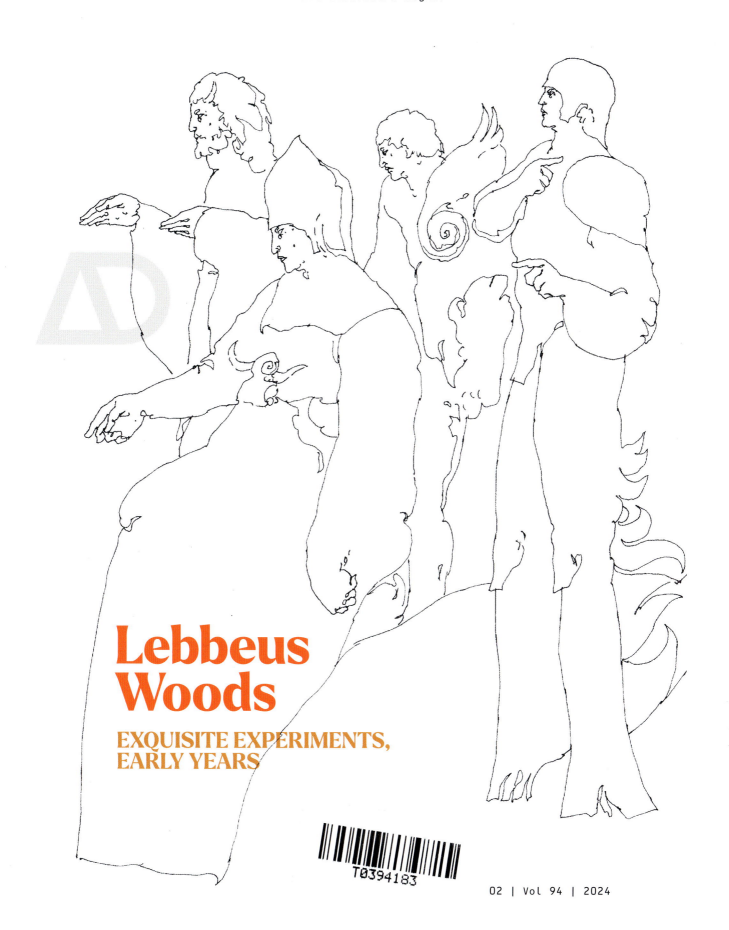

Lebbeus Woods

EXQUISITE EXPERIMENTS, EARLY YEARS

02 | Vol 94 | 2024

LEBBEUS WOODS:
EXQUISITE EXPERIMENTS, EARLY YEARS

About the   5
Editors

Neil Spiller and Aleksandra Wagner

Introduction   6

A Fecund Lucidity

Spadework for a Palace

Neil Spiller and Aleksandra Wagner

Self-Portrait with   14
Burned Weapon

The Wound That
Does Not Heal

Mark Dorrian

Inventing the World   22

In and Around Illinois,
1960–75

Sharon Irish

From Experimental   30
**Epistemology
to Experimental
Architecture**

Ben Sweeting

Framing the Sky,   38
Etching Clay

Walls of the Midwest

Kevin Erickson

Lebbeus – A   48
Postmodernist?

Early Scenes of Shopping
and Dwelling

Aaron Betsky

Attuned Rigour   58

Between Pictorial and
Material Conditions

Riet Eeckhout

ISSN 0003-8504   ISBN 978 1 119 98430 6

Edited by **Neil Spiller and Aleksandra Wagner**

Magical Transubstantiations 68
A Voyage to Italy

Aleksandra Wagner and Neil Spiller

Polymorphic Matters 102
Architecture, Change and Imagination

Ashley Simone

Exit Velocity 110
Einstein Tomb

Joseph Becker

Catalytic Moments, Friendships and Journeys 118

Peter Cook

Myth and Measure 74
Drawings of the 1970s

Lawrence Rinder

'The notion of "early years" – a search for modes of thought and for techniques that would make such thoughts readable – has an aura of excitement and discovery, combined with a youthful productivity of output'

— Neil Spiller and Aleksandra Wagner

Post-Apocalypse 84
The 'Ring' Cycle

Jörg H Gleiter

From Another Perspective

The Samizdats 128
Subversive Polemic

Neil Spiller

In Place of Light 92
On Early Writings

Eliyahu Keller

Contributors 134

Editorial Offices
John Wiley & Sons
9600 Garsington Road
Oxford
OX4 2DQ

T +44 (0)18 6577 6868

Editor
Neil Spiller

Managing Editor
Caroline Ellerby
Caroline Ellerby Publishing

Freelance Contributing Editor
Abigail Grater

Publisher
Todd Green

Art Direction + Design
Christian Küsters
Mihaela Mincheva
CHK Design

Production Editor
Elizabeth Gongde

Prepress
Artmedia, London

Printed in the United Kingdom
by Hobbs the Printers Ltd

Front cover
Lebbeus Woods,
Untitled, 1970s.
© Photo Clara Syme / a83

Inside front cover
Lebbeus Woods,
Quadrapolar distortions: violation of the second law, 'Cycles of Unity', *c* 1985.
© The Estate of Lebbeus Woods

Page 1
Lebbeus Woods,
Drawing from Black Notebook #20, 21 April 1976 (detail).
© The Estate of Lebbeus Woods

EDITORIAL BOARD

Denise Bratton
Paul Brislin
Mark Burry
Helen Castle
Nigel Coates
Peter Cook
Kate Goodwin
Edwin Heathcote
Brian McGrath
Jayne Merkel
Peter Murray
Mark Robbins
Deborah Saunt
Patrik Schumacher
Jill Stoner
Ken Yeang

Disclaimer
The Publisher and Editors cannot be held responsible for errors or any consequences arising from the use of information contained in this journal; the views and opinions expressed do not necessarily reflect those of the Publisher and Editors, neither does the publication of advertisements constitute any endorsement by the Publisher and Editors of the products advertised.

ARCHITECTURAL DESIGN
March/April 2024
Volume 94
Issue 02

Journal Customer Services
For ordering information, claims and any enquiry concerning your journal subscription please go to www.wileycustomerhelp.com/ask or contact your nearest office.

Americas
E: cs-journals@wiley.com
T: +1 877 762 2974

Europe, Middle East and Africa
E: cs-journals@wiley.com
T: +44 (0)1865 778 315

Asia Pacific
E: cs-journals@wiley.com
T: +65 6511 8000

Japan (for Japanese-speaking support)
E: cs-japan@wiley.com
T: +65 6511 8010

Visit our Online Customer Help available in 7 languages at www.wileycustomerhelp.com/ask

Print ISSN: 0003-8504
Online ISSN: 1554-2769

All prices are subject to change without notice.

Identification Statement
Periodicals Postage paid at Rahway, NJ 07065. Air freight and mailing in the USA by Mercury Media Processing, 1850 Elizabeth Avenue, Suite C, Rahway, NJ 07065, USA.

USA Postmaster
Please send address changes to *Architectural Design*, John Wiley & Sons Inc., c/o The Sheridan Press, PO Box 465, Hanover, PA 17331, USA

Rights and Permissions
Requests to the Publisher should be addressed to:
Permissions Department
John Wiley & Sons Ltd
The Atrium
Southern Gate
Chichester
West Sussex PO19 8SQ
UK

F: +44 (0)1243 770 620
E: Permissions@wiley.com

All Rights Reserved. No part of this publication may be reproduced, stored in a retrieval system or transmitted in any form or by any means, electronic, mechanical, photocopying, recording, scanning or otherwise, except under the terms of the Copyright, Designs and Patents Act 1988 or under the terms of a licence issued by the Copyright Licensing Agency Ltd, 5th Floor, Shackleton House, Battle Bridge Lane, London SE1 2HX, without the permission in writing of the Publisher.

△ is published bimonthly and is available to purchase as individual volumes at the following prices.

Individual copies:
£29.99 / US$45.00
Mailing fees for print may apply

ABOUT THE EDITORS

NEIL SPILLER AND ALEKSANDRA WAGNER

Editor of 🅐 Neil Spiller considered Lebbeus Woods a friend, a mentor, and a fellow traveller with whom he shared spaces of architectural discourse, a high regard for the medium of drawing, and a deep affinity for experimentation and teaching. He considers it a great honour to have co-edited, with Aleksandra Wagner, this unique publication based on explorations of the richness of the Lebbeus Woods Archive.

Neil was Visiting Professor of Architecture at Carleton University in Ottawa, Canada (2020–22), and Visiting Professor at IAUV Venice in 2021. He was previously Hawksmoor Chair of Architecture and Landscape and Deputy Pro Vice-Chancellor of the University of Greenwich, London. Prior to this he was Dean of the School of Architecture, Design and Construction and Professor of Architecture and Digital Theory at Greenwich, and Vice-Dean and Graduate Director of Design at the Bartlett School of Architecture, University College London (UCL).

He has guest-edited eight 🅐 issues, including the highly successful *Architects in Cyberspace I* and *II* (1995 and 1998) and *Drawing Architecture* (2013), and more recently edited the issues *Emerging Talents: Training Architects* (July/August 2021), *Radical Architectural Drawing* (July/August 2022), *California Dreaming* (March/April 2023) and *A Sublime Synthesis: Architecture and Art* (September/October 2023).

His books include *Visionary Architecture: Blueprints of the Modern Imagination* (2006), *Educating Architects* (2014) and *Architecture and Surrealism* (2016), all published by Thames & Hudson. He is also the author of *How to Thrive in Architecture School: A Student Guide* (RIBA, 2020).

Aleksandra Wagner is a psychoanalyst, and Professor Emerita at The New School in New York City. She is a training and supervising analyst and faculty at the city's National Psychological Association for Psychoanalysis (NPAP) and at the China American Psychoanalytic Alliance (CAPA), and the Interim Editor of *The Psychoanalytic Review*. She is the editor of the *Shame* special issue of *Cabinet* magazine (2008), and co-editor of *Considering Forgiveness* (Vera List Center for Art and Politics, 2009) and *Lebbeus Woods: Zagreb Free Zone Revisited* (ORIS House of Architecture and Faculty of Architecture, University of Zagreb, 2021). She translated Lebbeus Woods's *War and Architecture* (1993) into Serbo-Croatian, and co-edited and co-translated the *Sarajevo Survival Guide* (Workman Publishing, 1993) into English. She is the Executor of the Estate of Lebbeus Woods. 🅐

Text © 2024 John Wiley & Sons Ltd. Images: (t) © Robbie Munn; (b) © Lydia Matthews

A FECUND LUCIDITY
SPADEWORK FOR A PALACE

INTRODUCTION

NEIL SPILLER AND
ALEKSANDRA WAGNER

Lebbeus Woods,
Untitled,
1970s

A pensive figure engaged in their labour. An alchemist? An astronomer? A sculptor? Or simply an ink and marker on board with collage?

Since my earliest involvement with architecture and art I have been concerned with finding the architectonic, design means for expressing [to] myself and others both those timeless qualities of the human mind – found in the noble and perfect forms of mathematics, geometry, and works of art and architecture we call classical – and the ephemeral qualities of mind derived from moment to moment experience and found anywhere, everywhere – epitomized perhaps in the great urban centers, the cities, where there is no perfection, only a continuum, an evolution of myriad forms. These are paradoxical qualities and lay foundation for an inner human conflict and struggle from which human creativity is born.
— Lebbeus Woods, 1974[1]

In a succinct and lucid entry in one of his 'Black Notebooks', written in June 1974, Lebbeus Woods – then 34 – describes what became a series of architectural and artistic preoccupations that sustained a lifetime's creative career. Some of these are spelled out through prose (diaristic, reflecting on art and architecture, as well as fiction), myth-research and myth-making or polemical passages on the state of the field; others through inquiry into potentials of visual imagination. The unifying strand is the record of an extraordinary deftness and variety – technical as well as conceptual – with which Woods expresses his fecund ideas. The quoted paragraph encapsulates and interpolates his interest in the roots of architectural discourse and its intersection with the arresting complexities of the great chunking engine of the city.

Woods also articulates his understanding of the importance of transience and fluidity – conditions of modernity. Never conflict-free, they all enable, even require, rejoicing in differences between individual actors and the ways they construct realities based on their conversation with, and an awareness of, what surrounds them – physically, emotionally and intellectually.

In the Beginning
The notion of 'early years' – a search for modes of thought and for techniques that would make such thoughts readable – has an aura of excitement and discovery, combined with a youthful productivity of output. Lebbeus Woods's 'juvenilia', if one may call it that, is a painstaking celebration of personal liberation through the habits of thinking, writing and drawing. The outcomes are both unsettled and unsettling, but are always motile and appear assured. This has prompted some to ask (as early or as late as the mid-1980s): How did he arrive on the 'scene' so fully formed, from 'nowhere'?

One manner of answering involves a good dose of literalness, nearly an agreement with the imperial tone addressed to the 'nowhere': from 'the lost region'[2] of the American Midwest, and from the then less-than-fashionable quarters in and out of New York City. Another (addressed to the 'how') offers a chance to be more psychologically, even professionally, astute: by way of solitude – sometimes contextual, but more often a result of self-imposed discipline.

Yet, the real weight may be in different questions: What constitutes the 'scene' from which the accounting starts? What 'scenes' were there before?

Most architects have a 'family tree' that can be traced back through genealogies of tutors, mentors or influential practitioners. Woods appears to be an exception in this regard, insofar as he never spells out his influences in a singular, cogent statement. Still, the famed trope, 'anxiety of influence',[3] does not apply. Woods's deep interest in the achievements of others – not necessarily all architects – is inked in his notebooks and on the loose pages of his unpublished early writings. For attentive interpreters, influences are also evident in the work that marks him as a proponent of a particular kind of visual sensibility. This world – Woods's world – is predicated on the will to find out 'what if'.

Lost and Found
Luckily, many of the tracings of the early moments have survived, to marvel at, enjoy and speculate about. Though Woods's later oeuvre has been widely exhibited, published and acclaimed, his early work was rarely shown, mostly in the time closer to its origin, and without publications that would offer another layer of meaning. When seen through his Archive – in conversation with what came later – it points to the same energetic mind, eye and hand, prone to risk-taking. This ⌀ seeks to bring to a wider international audience a few of these exquisite experiments, by having them discussed from a variety of perspectives. Some of the contributors were colleagues and friends of Lebbeus Woods; others met the work without ever meeting its creator. Some faced what Woods himself may have maintained – that 'the past is a foreign country';[4] others have been keen to recognise lasting continuities.

Spanning the period between the late 1960s and 1985, the works and the attendant critical discourse are only partially set out in the chronological order in which they were made. The collection of articles commences with an eloquent introduction to the existence of the Black Notebooks that Woods kept in the 1970s, by Mark Dorrian, Forbes Chair in Architecture at the University of Edinburgh, UK. The Black Notebooks' meticulousness reveals a young man sometimes prone to despair. Dorrian's piece centres around an enigmatic self-portrait, from which he extrapolates both Woods's complexity as a person and his graphic industriousness.

The Midwest

As Woods advocated all his life, the notion of where one lives, and how one interacts with one's location and community, organises who one becomes. The formation is an ever-dynamic, evolving process. Woods spent a number of his early years in Urbana-Champaign, Illinois, in America's Midwest – not in the hustle and bustle of the academic and urban metropolises – although it was Manhattan where he anchored the second half of his life.

Urbana-Champaign are two contiguous municipalities dominated by the large and lively public University of Illinois; Woods studied architecture there. Architectural historian Sharon Irish situates some of Woods's early contacts and influences – his mentors of urbanity – through this lens. Ben Sweeting, who teaches architecture at the University of Brighton, UK, explores the flowering of one of the most profound encounters and friendships Woods had whilst still an architecture student, with scientist and cyberneticist Heinz von Foerster. Their exchanges sparked and sustained Woods's lifelong interest in cybernetics, documented in the drawings Woods did for von Foerster's papers, but also in his overall approach to the practice of architecture.

Lebbeus Woods,
Gray Works,
1976–8

left: A quiet study of light and darkness, the ultimate media of life and of architecture.

Lebbeus Woods,
Waiting for Odysseus,
1975

below: Photo by Lebbeus Woods of a forlorn parking lot in Champaign, Illinois, with the wall where he will draw his *Odysseus*.

Architect and University of Illinois associate professor Kevin Erickson examines the built and natural topology of the Midwest – a land of few walls – and comments on two of Woods's local 'Wall' projects. Aaron Betsky, a professor in the School of Architecture and Design at Virginia Tech in Blacksburg, Virginia, asks the question: Was Woods a Postmodernist? He substantiates his arguments by addressing the work from the early to mid-1970s, including the first significant acknowledgment Woods received: the Progressive Architecture Award of 1974.

Elective Affinities
Riet Eeckhout, a guest professor and post-doctoral researcher at the faculty of architecture of KU Leuven, Belgium, explores Woods's experimentation with differing surfaces and treatments of representation through the media of Mylar polyester film and oil pastels. Continuing the theme of drawing, the Guest-Editors follow Woods's Italian journey of 1978, and his ability to weave the varied patterns, building typologies and synthesis of art, sculpture and architecture into his own work. The sojourn continues through the contribution by Lawrence Rinder, Director Emeritus of the University of California, Berkeley Art Museum and Pacific Film Archive, who determines a resonance between the 18th-century Venetian painter and printmaker Giambattista Tiepolo and Woods's output – particularly in relation to the depiction of the human/mythic figure.

As Woods advocated all his life, the notion of where one lives, and how one interacts with one's location and community, organises who one becomes. The formation is an ever–dynamic, evolving process

Lebbeus Woods,
Painting on textile,
24 January 1976

A rare experiment by Woods of painting on muslin.

Lebbeus Woods,
Drawing from 'The Four Houses',
1975

The 12-drawing portfolio 'The Four Houses' was conceptualised as a series of visual essays – an allegory of change, an epistemological quadripartite macrocosm. In the language of Woods, each House is seen as existing in a timeless mythic world, each the temple of a different stage of human epic.

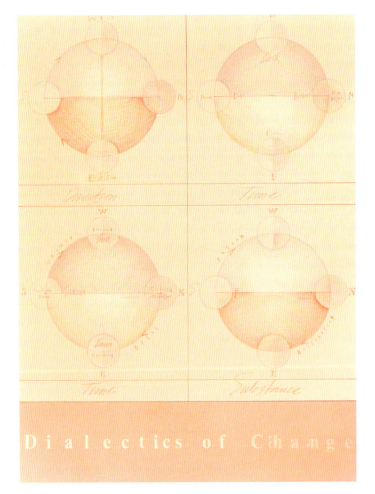

Lebbeus Woods,
Dialectics of Change,
'The Four Houses',
1975

Some works in the series, like this one, have enigmatic titles such as *The Great Tension, Form as Meta (form/phor)* and *Four Corners of the World*.

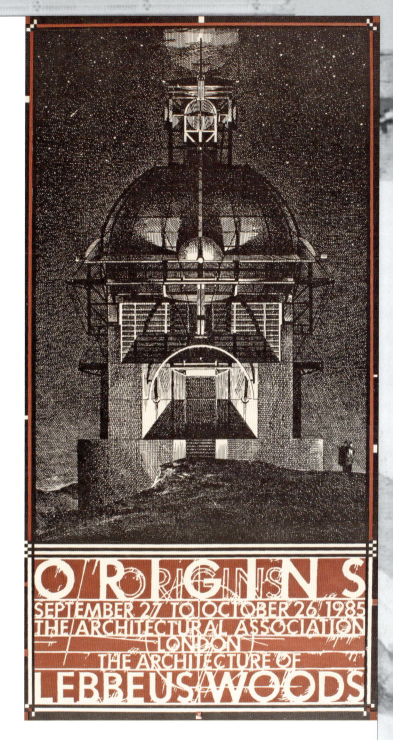

Lebbeus Woods,
Poster for the 'Origins'
exhibition at the
Architectural Association (AA)
School of Architecture,
London,
1985

Poster designed by Woods with an image of his *Epicyclarium*, a project 'conceived as a cure for fever – a fever to build'.

While these themes may be new to those who have encountered Lebbeus Woods and his work after the mid-1980s, even less known may be his affinity with the 19th-century German composer Richard Wagner and especially his opera cycle *Der Ring des Nibelungen* (*The Ring of the Nibelung*, 1848–74). Jörg H Gleiter, an architect and Professor of Architectural Theory at the Technical University Berlin, introduces us to the anatomy and mythology of Wagner's operas, and to Woods's drawn response. In Gleiter's interpretation, both Woods's and Wagner's works are post-apocalyptic visions, evoking the calm after the storm and the birth of a very different dawn.

Eliyahu Keller, an assistant professor in the Faculty of Architecture and Town Planning at the Technion – Israel Institute of Technology, Haifa, investigates Woods's early written work (emergence of a writerly voice) and its calligraphic intent (texts treated as drawings). He also focuses on Woods's use of light and darkness, conveyed at the intersection between drawings and thought.

Space-Time Continuum
Ashley Simone, an associate professor at the Pratt Institute School of Architecture in New York City, explores time, change and polymorphism in Woods's oeuvre, and particularly his 'AEON' project (1979–85) – consisting of four cities, each dedicated to one of the elements (air, water, earth, fire). This overarching epistemological quadripartite macrocosm, Woods believed, could also be seen in the microcosms – always soft binaries – of men and women, life and death, nature and technology.

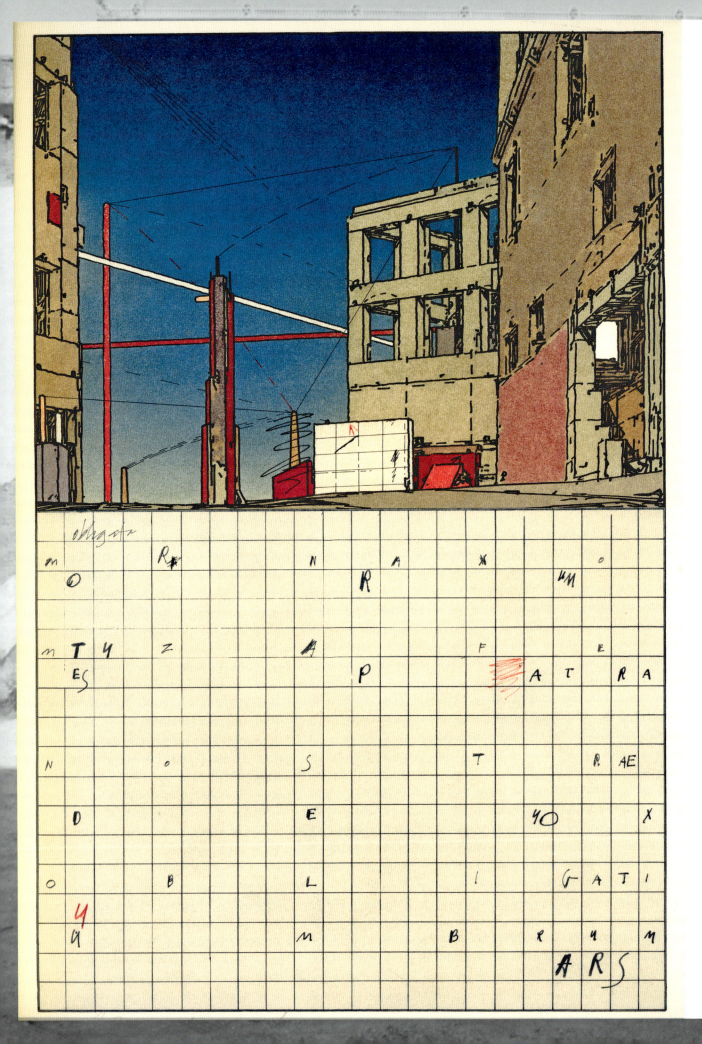

In 1985, London's Architectural Association (AA) School of Architecture held an exhibition titled 'Lebbeus Woods: Origins'. The show announced to the architectural world a breath of fresh air

Lebbeus Woods, Drawing from *Architecture-Sculpture-Painting*, 1979

'My drawings are executed in several media and are divided among notebooks and portfolios, appearing to comprise many different series, but actually amounting to the elaboration of a single idea: the integration of painting, art and architecture' (p 2).

Notes
1. Lebbeus Woods, Black Notebook #12, 13 October 1973 – 6/7 June 1974 (entry of 2 June 1974), unpaginated, Lebbeus Woods Archive.
2. See Jon K Lauck, *The Lost Region: Toward a Revival of Midwestern History*, University of Iowa Press (Iowa City), 2013.
3. See Harold Bloom, *The Anxiety of Influence: A Theory of Poetry*, Oxford University Press (New York), 1973.
4. The popular phrase coined in the opening words of LP Hartley, *The Go-Between*, Hamish Hamilton (London), 1953.
5. Lebbeus Woods, *Pamphlet Architecture 6: Einstein Tomb*, William Stout Publishers (San Francisco), 1980, unpaginated.
6. *Lebbeus Woods: Origins*, exhibition catalogue, AA Publications (London), 1985, p 4.
7. László Krasznahorkai, *Spadework for a Palace: Entering the Madness of Others* [2018], tr John Batki, New Directions Publishing (New York), 2022, p 58.
8. DW Winnicott, *The Maturational Process and the Facilitating Environment*, International University Press (New York), 1965, p 187.

Joseph Becker, Associate Curator of Architecture and Design at the San Francisco Museum of Modern Art (SFMOMA), ponders the horizon of one of Woods's most iconic early projects, *Einstein Tomb* (1979–80). A cenotaph for the great physicist of relativity – bound by, and unbound from, gravity – *Einstein Tomb* was a response to the *architecture parlante* (literally 'speaking architecture') of the visionary 18th-century French Enlightenment architects Claude-Nicholas Ledoux and Étienne-Louis Boullée, a passage of ideas and of architecture 'under the vagrant light of stars'.[5]

In September–October 1985, London's Architectural Association (AA) School of Architecture held an exhibition titled 'Lebbeus Woods: Origins'. The show announced to the architectural world a breath of fresh air. Peter Cook – co-founder of avant-garde 1960s architecture group Archigram and later Chair at the Bartlett School of Architecture, University College London – wrote an introduction to its catalogue.[6] His contribution in this volume charts some of the memories of their alliance and their friendship.

The final reflection concerns Woods's self-published pamphlets (1976–9), the samizdats. These missives, whose interlocutors we are left to imagine, were made to propagate his select works at the time when a Post Office (or a private delivery) was still a standard mode of communication.

Reality Is No Obstacle
In his book *Spadework for a Palace* (2018), Hungarian writer László Krasznahorkai makes Lebbeus Woods meet the American novelist Herman Melville (1819–1891) and English poet and novelist Malcolm Lowry (1909–1957), both walkers through the city. Krasznahorkai writes of Woods's ideas as 'not so much about architecture but about thinking itself, about the ways in which we *could* think about architecture, and along with that, about things in general, recognizing the essence of the subject in a way that no one ever had before, so that now we may begin to talk about this essence, or in his case, make drawings about it.'[7] This 𝕯 charts some of Woods's attempts to glean that essence himself, allowing readers to see what may have led to it.

We thank all the contributors, whose enthusiasm remains an inspiration. Their attentive use of the Lebbeus Woods Archive in New York City and patience through the subsequent email exchanges provided valuable clarifications. Given its size, this volume can serve merely as a signpost for research directions yet to be taken. With a nod to psychoanalyst Donald Woods Winnicott's much-quoted pronouncement that 'It is joy to be hidden but disaster not to be found',[8] we hope that the vitality of Lebbeus Woods's early work – the lucidity of his experiments – shines out of this publication. 𝕯

Text © 2024 John Wiley & Sons Ltd. Images: © The Estate of Lebbeus Woods

Mark Dorrian

Self-Portrait with Burned Weapon

The Wound That Does Not Heal

Setting aside organic metaphors of growth and maturation, architect and author **Mark Dorrian** addresses the 'early work' by attending to Lebbeus Woods's descriptively yet evocatively named Black Notebooks. Turning his mind's eye to the Notebooks as a record of the interior struggles of their author — as spiritual diaries — he takes on the symbolism of the wound that must be suffered, and finds much that sheds light on the younger Woods and on his lasting ambitions for architecture.

```
Lebbeus Woods,
Self-Portrait with Burned Weapon,
Black Notebook #16,
6 April 1975
```

A drawing that comes at the end of a sequence linked to Richard Wagner's *Parsifal*. It begins with a drawing of Amfortas, who suffers a wound that will not heal.

Inevitably, in one sense at least, early work arrives late. For it gains its particular meaning and status only when we are directed to it by subsequent 'mature' productions, which, by forming an interpretative context for what has come before, place demands upon it. Typically, the 'early' is examined for intimations of what will emerge, and given importance insofar as it displays these. Indeed, it is difficult to see how work that showed no discernible connections of this kind could be described as 'early' at all. Approaches of this sort are implicitly teleological – the value of early work is established on its documentation of the development of the artist who is bound to arise; it is juvenilia whose unnecessary features will wither away to release the work into what it had to become.

But this is not the only way to think. Another would be to set aside organic metaphors of growth and maturation, and look instead for a differential pattern of potentials and possibilities that, while sharing affinities, do not imply a single, inevitable future. This allows us to attend to early work in a different way, opening questions of what it did not – or even 'failed to' – become. The title of an early drawing series, 'Lost and Found' (1973), which Lebbeus Woods partially reprised many years later on his online blog, hints at something like this – a more discontinuous process of losing and finding (actions neither arbitrary nor unmotivated, this further complicating the relations between 'early' and 'late'). Of it, he wrote: 'What is interesting – and a little frightening – is that the basic forms and ideas were there from the beginning.'[1]

The notebooks also join a tradition of spiritual diaries, records of the interior struggles and self-exhortations of their author

Xenographics

The aim here is to explore some manifestations of the early work of Lebbeus Woods, trying to draw out aspects of the architect's thought that were – to me, at least – unexpected and different in kind from the usual narratives given. My sources are a limited number of the 'Black Notebooks' that Woods kept in the 1970s. The notebook as an object, an object that was also an idea, clearly held a special meaning for him. Tied to his long-standing sense of itinerancy, the notebooks are portable and mobile, while also offering, as he later said, a home and space of safety.[2] Their regular 11 x 14 inch format provides a constant that survives the frequently changing addresses written in their inner covers, the tension between the two reaching a height in the inscription for Black Notebook #16: 'Lebbeus Woods < No address at present > Call collect (317) 255-7066 if found.' This seems as much a statement of principle or an epigram as a declaration of fact. He assumes Xenon (Greek for 'stranger') as a persona, contemplates wandering 'the great cities an outcast, a stranger to their multitudes',[3] and adopts the monogrammatic X – the mark that is the sign of the mark itself, the minimal index of an anonymous presence. Complex artefacts – spaces of drawing and delineation, and of the written elaboration of ideas – the notebooks also join a tradition of spiritual diaries, records of the interior struggles and self-exhortations of their author. In this, they are powerful instruments of auto-construction, in which the self is reflected, explores its identity, dwells on what it could become, but also confronts what it might not.

In the notebook-without-address we find a drawing titled *Self-Portrait with Burned Weapon* (1975). A figure looks out at us, his head tilted to one side. The vertical dark stick that is in his hand (is the 'burned weapon' charcoal, and does the left hand indicate that this was drawn with a mirror?) could as easily be a nail driven through the finger as an implement grasped by it. What appears to be a sheet of paper in front of the figure is blank, but the surface that supports it is inscribed with a line and then a flurry of other marks. These reappear, seemingly as wounds, streaming from the hand that grasps – or is fixed by – the weapon and also the upper arm. The drawing comes after a sequence of images that begins with a small drawing of a man outlined in a square frame, his head occluded by shadow, his wrists bound in barbed wire, and a bleeding gash on his chest. Below we read 'Amfortas', the character from Richard Wagner's opera *Parsifal* (premiered 1882) who has been stabbed by the spear that pierced Christ's side, leaving an agonising wound that can only be healed by an 'innocent fool' who wields again the weapon. The next page seems to reprise the image, now as a helmeted figure engirdled with, once more, barbed wire. Then comes a frame with a face, and then a gaping visage with 'Fool' inscribed below.

In this sequence, are we looking at a series of self-portraits? Certainly, Woods strove for, as he wrote, 'integration' and 'coalescence', which could be understood as kinds of healing; and the sense of being wounded – indeed, of the wound as being the source of his work – recurs in his thinking. In a remarkable page, its text set out in a T-shape like a tau cross, he writes: 'An interlude of one / week, then vehemence; / The wounds split wide'.[4] Later, in a reflection on poetry and architecture, he states that his work 'is not poetry: it is a symbol of poetry. It is not a symbol but a wound, a cry of mingled joy and pain found upon my pages'.[5]

Lebbeus Woods,
Fire of the Inner City 3,
Black Notebook #12,
25 May 1974

Part of a series of drawings initiated with one titled *The Paradox of Warring Cities*.

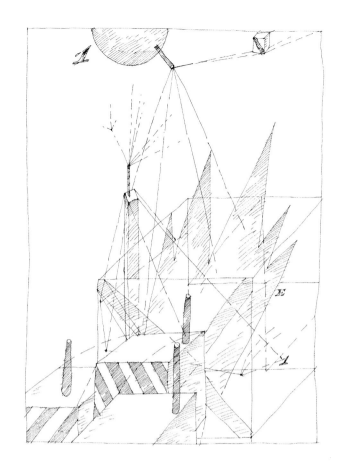

Lebbeus Woods,
Textual drawing from
Black Notebook #16,
14 April 1975

'The wounds split wide'. A textual drawing in the form of a tau cross.

AN INTERLUDE OF ONE WEEK, THEN VEHEMENCE; THE WOUNDS SPLIT WIDE,

MY FAULT IS GREAT; TO FORGIVE MYSELF FOR WEAKNESSES THAT I DID NOT KNOW: THE TASK AHEAD. ALONE, NOW...

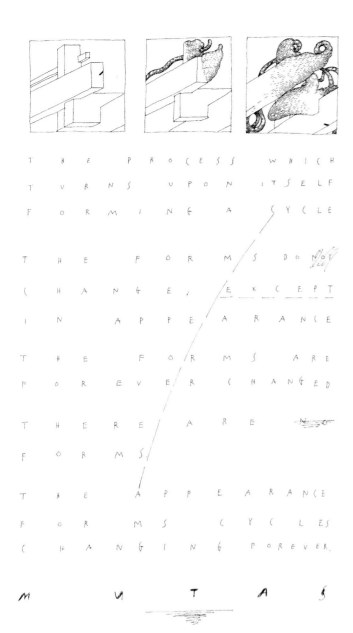

Lebbeus Woods,
Mutas,
Black Notebook #16,
19 April 1975

Coming after a declaration that 'The creation of symbols representative of a meaning to existence is the great task of the arts in any culture including our own', this image-text places its negatives 'under erasure'. The three images at the top relate to the 'Lost and Found' drawing series (1973).

The Architect as Symbolist

Opening Woods's notebooks, one is struck by the page composition, the precision with which the image is placed on the sheet, intensified by its framing and sometimes by the blocking-in of the framed area with a tonal wash. This can give the sense of looking through an aperture rather than at something on the page. Notwithstanding the priority he gave to the nonconceptual, to the spontaneous and the found, there is a powerful deliberativeness. He would later write: 'the contents of the notebook are not "sketches", preliminary attempts that will be finished later, but finished works in themselves'.[6] The spacing and arrangement of texts often share in this, taking on distinct spatial and architectonic qualities that seem close to Symbolist predecessors like the French poet Stéphane Mallarmé (1842–1898). Vectors, or perhaps trajectories, come to traverse and dynamise the textual surface, and text combines with image to produce an array of oracular icono-textual symbolisations. While these certainly have a foot in the modern modalities of the film storyboard or comic strip, they also appear to reach back to the word-and-image combinations of the artist William Blake (1757–1827) and to doctrines of the symbol as revelation that pass to Woods through sources such as the book *A Vision* (1925)[7] by the Anglo-Irish poet William Butler Yeats, whose occult thinking at this point permeates the architect's ideas.

For Woods, the epochal task of any art, and indeed of a life, is the forging of symbols: 'to reach that plane', he wrote, 'to fulfill my mind and body, to wrench the symbols of unity from the grasp of the unknown and return with them to light constitute a single journey, whose vehicle is drawing'.[8] This is a search for 'wholeness of being' and it is the privileged role of the symbol to act as its monument and threshold. Woods finds contemporary treatments of 'symbolic architecture' bifurcated and inadequate to his conception of the symbol – he drafts a letter to a journal that had published some postmodern houses and writes a response to Christian Norberg-Schulz's *Intentions in Architecture* (1965)[9] ('his theory is not so much untrue as it is half-true'), finding that both neglect the awful fervour of Dionysian life forces.[10]

The priority Woods ascribes to the symbol arises against a background of necessary conflict. It is the symbol's task to express and transcend the conflict in an apprehension of coalescence, a heterogeneous unity on a higher plane that is unavailable to the differential structuring of rational thought. Woods historically associates this revelation of totality through the symbol with ritual and religious experience, although in the late modern context the search is an individual one undertaken under a condition of 'personal power' exerted in the face of stifling group institutions.[11] There is a markedly countercultural mood to his thinking here.

The architect's reflections on conflict were shaped by interlocutors who were informed by the philosophy of Friedrich Nietzsche, such as Yeats and the Greek writer Nikos Kazantzakis (1883–1957). Through geometric-rational and animalistic-serpentine forms, drawings in the 'Lost and Found' series had explored the interplay of Apollonian serenity and Dionysian turbulence. This was further developed in the extensive drawings and notes for the 'Four Houses' series (1975), which reworked the lunar Great Wheel of Yeats's *A Vision*, and his idea of antithetical impulses that wax and wane according to the interaction of vortex-like 'gyres', as a cyclic journey between opposed conditions of intellect and will.

Lebbeus Woods,
Arkos: Towards a Civilization 79,
Black Notebook #12,
12 March 1974

A layout for a comic-strip-like panel, perhaps linked to the reflection at the start of the notebook: 'For now then – what works can I do for others? ... A poster, then, to architects whose work reflects an interest in a union of painting and architecture'.

Lebbeus Woods,
Textual drawing from Black Notebook #16,
6 April 1975

From a series of concise poetic texts, with small emblem-like drawings.

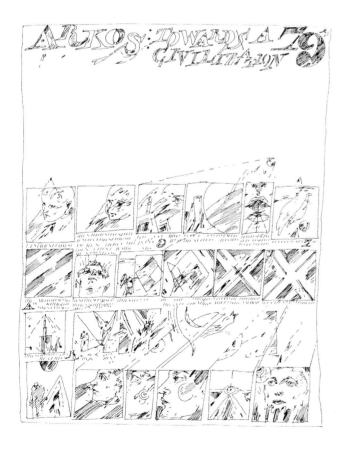

Woods restated this in various ways. In one account, intellect (which is creative and commands the power of symbolisation, although sterile without the will) and will (a condition of pure sensation and affective energies) are understood to enact a kind of violence upon themselves, this producing the torsion of the circuit. Through its abstraction of matter, the intellect ultimately negates itself, while the will's incorporative appetites lead to the dissolution of its own boundaries, propelling it toward the intellect. Most important for Woods were what he calls the 'balance' points, at which art can wrest some kind of momentary totality. Within this system, four locations on the cycle – intellect; ironic balance (intellect's passage to its submergence in will); will; and heroic balance (will's movement toward intellect) – became metaphysical cardinal points, sites for 'temples' as Woods called them, which he drew in a play of destruction and recomposition.[12]

As intellect falls into and dissolves in the will, it deposits the broken remains of its prior symbols in the latter's domain, which await discovery like – Woods suggested – the chthonic antique ruins that animated the Renaissance. Perhaps it is this condition of vestigial survival and haunting that was articulated when he wrote: 'In my dominion, which is a ruined temple, there are creatures only half-formed by outer civilizations. Past the cities, or rather beneath them, are ancestral realms unlike graveyards, distant even from underworlds.'[13] It is likely that this sense of

As intellect falls into and dissolves in the will, it deposits the broken remains of its prior symbols in the latter's domain

Lebbeus Woods,
Spread with notes and diagrams
for the 'Four Houses' (1975),
Black Notebook #16,
25 April 1975

'These drawings', Woods writes, 'must be seen as testament of one mind's quest for wholeness through the expression of all perceptions and ideas contending continually within it'. The main diagram tabulates the relations that correspond to each of the four 'cardinal' positions on the Wheel.

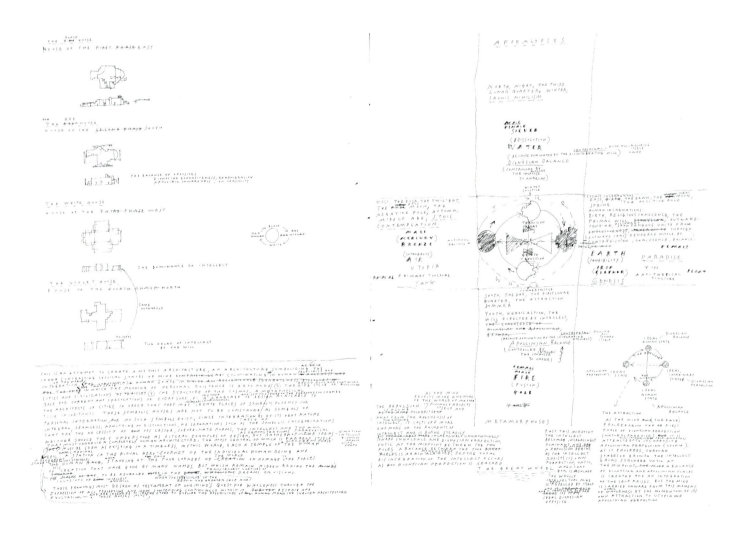

conflictual combination and co-presence underpinned Woods's fascination with animal-human hybrids, which, despite his avowed appreciation for the work of the German artist Max Ernst (1891–1976), seem more like *emblemata* than Surrealist monsters; likely too, that his search for symbols able to both encompass and unify conflict underlay his euphoric response to experiments using transparent Mylar to produce, through bilateral symmetries, fluctuating alternations between a-formality and geometric effect.

The Patch

And yet, despite the excitement of such discoveries, it seems that a constant sense of despair haunted Woods's project of symbology. Perhaps this was to do with an understanding that the symbol, by his own account, was fated always to remain on the side of the intellect, drawing up to the edge of an abyss that must remain unknowable and unnameable. For while only extra-rational inspiration could grasp truth, 'all symbols [must remain] devices of the intellect only, while integration is of the whole being'.[14] It is a despair that flickers throughout the notebooks and that one senses even in – maybe especially in – their moments of heightened affirmation.

Seen in this way, the symbol looks less like transcendence than a symptom of desire for it – a patch that is placed on top of a wound it cannot close over and must be suffered, unhealed, below. ᗯ

Notes
1. Lebbeus Woods, '1 January 21, 2008: Lost and Found', in Clare Jacobson (ed), *Slow Manifesto: Lebbeus Woods Blog*, Princeton Architectural Press (New York), 2015, p 16.
2. Lebbeus Woods, 'March 15, 2009: Notebook 97-3', in *ibid*, p 67.
3. Lebbeus Woods, Black Notebook #16, 6 April – 3 May 1975 (entry of 25 April), unpaginated, Lebbeus Woods Archive.
4. *Ibid*.
5. *Ibid*.
6. Woods, 'March 15, 2009: Notebook 97-3', *op cit*, p 67.
7. Privately published; see Catherine E Paul and Margaret Mills Harper (eds), *Collected Works of WB Yeats, Volume XIII: A Vision*, Scribner (New York), 2008.
8. Woods, Black Notebook #16, entry of 16 April.
9. Christian Norberg-Schulz, *Intentions in Architecture*, MIT Press (Cambridge, MA), 1965.
10. Woods, Black Notebook #16, entry of 3 May.
11. Lebbeus Woods, Black Notebook #12, entry of 2 June 1974 (entry of 27 April 1974), unpaginated, Lebbeus Woods Archive.
12. Woods, Black Notebook #16, entry of 3 May.
13. Woods, Black Notebook #12, entry of 6 June 1974.
14. Woods, Black Notebook #16, entry of 17 April'.

Lebbeus Woods, Drawing from Black Notebook #12, 6/7 June 1974

Bird-humans seem to honour ... whom? The architect, who presents to them an object like a feathered prayer stick? Given Woods's enthusiasm for Max Ernst, it might recall the Dada-Surrealist artist's avian familiar Loplop, 'bird superior'.

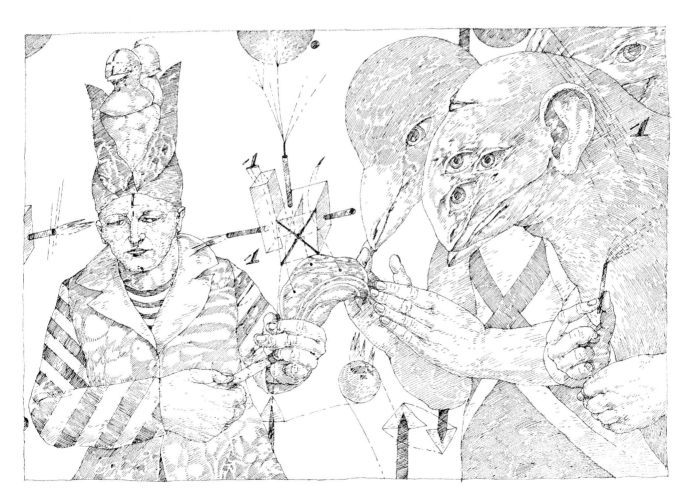

Text © 2024 John Wiley & Sons Ltd.
Images © The Estate of Lebbeus Woods. Lebbeus Woods Archive

Sharon Irish

Inventing the World

In and Around Illinois, 1960–75

```
Lebbeus Woods,
Studio sale poster,
1975
```

A portrait of an artist as a young man, on a poster designed by Woods announcing his studio sale in Champaign, Illinois. The highlighted theme of Cybernetic Circus combines two important influences, of cyberneticist Heinz von Foerster and architect A Richard Williams.

Some of Lebbeus Woods's formative years were spent on the 'flat, treeless plain' at the University of Illinois School of Architecture and at various home and studio addresses in Urbana–Champaign. Architectural historian Sharon Irish describes the dynamic setting of this urban stage and Woods's personal and professional preoccupations of the time.

In his 15 intermittent years in Urbana-Champaign, Lebbeus Woods moved from undergraduate student to award-winning design director, from skilful renderer to experimental architect. The grandeur of his ideas shaped this trajectory, which he articulated in a 1991 essay about what drove his work: '[T]o become part of the world I cannot merely represent it through critique or some kind of mimetic activity, but must invent the world. Not a world, not *my* world, but *the* world.'[1]

That world was charged with struggle and triumph. In an unpublished manuscript, 'Notes on the World Myth' (1970), Woods wrote that life was 'rich with blood and laughter, mystical, adventurous and ever-ragged at the edges'.[2] His energetic vision was at heart theatrical, a quality he explored with Illinois-based architect A Richard Williams, whose book *The Urban Stage* (1980)[3] included Woods's drawings, and whose mentorship gave Woods a sense of urban design and built spaces as settings for human drama. In part due to this influence, his aim became to create totalising environments that depicted such possibilities.

Harrison & Abramovitz,
Assembly Hall (now State Farm Center),
Champaign, Illinois,
1963

Designed by alumnus Max Abramovitz and his firm with Wallace K Harrison, Assembly Hall was built south of the University of Illinois proper, at a remove from the brick-and-stone Neo-Georgian architecture of central campus. This aerial view from the northwest shows the elegant folded-plate, edge-supported dome, which rests on a pre-stressed concrete ring of concrete buttresses that form the rim. Lebbeus Woods expressed admiration for the design in the student newspaper in 1964.

'The Flat, Treeless Plain' of Urbana-Champaign

The 20-year-old Lebbeus Woods arrived in east-central Illinois in 1960, from Indianapolis. He had studied engineering briefly at Purdue University after graduating from Shortridge High School in 1959. After coursework at Purdue from September 1959 to April 1960, he transferred to the University of Illinois Urbana-Champaign to study architecture. The only child of a West Point-trained civil engineer, Colonel Lebbeus Bigelow Woods, the younger Woods had grown up on military bases and then, after 1953, in Indianapolis with his widowed mother, Dorothy H Woods. In his blog, Woods recalled 'hanging out around jet aircraft and their pilots' at sites where his father worked. The first US human space flight with Alan Shepard occurred in 1961, helping to promote 'the technological spin-offs of the space programs, impacting society particularly in the development of telecommunications, computers and earth-satellites'.[4] Images of outer space and structures in flight appear frequently in Woods's work, extrapolating from his early exposure to these technologies.

The Urbana-Champaign campus of the University of Illinois featured mostly red brick buildings; many of them were conceived in a Georgian Revival style by Charles Platt in the 1920s. Former Illinois professor and Woods's one-time employer, Ambrose Richardson, described them as 'false-chimney architecture'.[5] In the early 1960s the campus was growing, with significant projects underway. The Illini Student Union was doubled in size; Assembly Hall, designed by Max Abramowitz, was completed in 1963; and the College of Education opened in 1964, after a design by A Richard Williams.

Woods published his views on Abramowitz's Assembly Hall in the student newspaper *The Daily Illini*, noting 'the incredible skill' of its construction, and continued: 'While little has been said in its favor, this building possesses a single fundamental virtue that makes its shortcomings insignificant; a completeness and unity of social intent and appropriateness of form to the demands of interior use and of the community life without.'[6] This brief opinion piece indicates Woods's awareness of the context of individual built structures; not only were they designed objects but they existed as part of 'community life' beyond their footprints.

According to his University of Illinois transcript, Woods excelled at architectural design and freehand drawing. By 1961 he had won an Earl Prize for excellence in undergraduate design.[7] He also took Air Force science, architectural history, physics, physical education, and materials and methods of construction – and received unremarkable grades. He dropped out of school in April of 1963 with 53 credits. Increasingly dissatisfied with academic work, he never completed his undergraduate degree.

Still, Woods drew and painted prolifically, for himself, on commission, and as an illustrator for hire. Even when his work was abstract, his sensibility was informed by real-life observation grounded in his immediate environment: 'Junk piles. I have always been fascinated by them, ever since, as a student, I was taken by a drawing teacher to some railroad yards in central Illinois. There were many things to draw in the landscape of tracks, roundhouses, sidetracked train cars (including long-empty living cars for railway workers), old and empty brick utility sheds, and the monumental cylindrical grain elevators lined up along the tracks, all of which had fallen into some state of disuse or abandonment, for reasons that were never clear. The flat, treeless plain on which these wonders lay was heavy with a feeling of something lost, but not dead, something living if only as a mystery.'[8]

Woods inhabited 'the flat, treeless plain' of central Illinois off and on from 1960 until 1975. Sometime in 1964, he moved with his family from Champaign to New York, where he worked for several years. Upon return to Champaign in 1967, he went to work until 1972 for Richardson, Severns, Scheeler and Associates (RSSA) on the design of the Indianapolis Museum of Art. From 1972 to 1975 he was director of design at Illinois Design Solutions (IDS, Inc). Woods shifted among corporate architecture, small regional design firms, freelance rendering jobs, art exhibitions and

During his time as a student at the University of Illinois, Woods encountered two men who had a distinct influence on him: Heinz von Foerster and A Richard Williams

Lebbeus Woods,
Promotional postcard,
c 1970

This postcard, dated 27 August 1970, was sent to Heinz von Foerster, who served as a reference for Woods as he tried to get illustration jobs. Woods used pen and ink to depict an austere *vanitas* tableau: a human skull rests atop a tangle of foliage emerging from a rectangular box.

Lebbeus Woods,
Page one of letter to A Richard Williams,
19 November 1970

Woods and his mentor at the University of Illinois, architect A Richard Williams, exchanged letters and personal visits. This first page of the letter here reflects on presentations about an environmental design conference held at the Center for Advanced Study at Illinois. Woods reports being 'struck' by the expressed need for an 'essential experience', attained 'in acts of the most sublime simplicity and directness'.

sales, and attempts to get grant funding to support himself and his family. He moved frequently within Urbana-Champaign, noting various addresses in his Notebooks.

Mentors of Urbanity

During his time as a student at the University of Illinois, Woods encountered two men who had a distinct influence on him: Heinz von Foerster and A Richard Williams. The cyberneticist von Foerster and Woods met through von Foerster's son, Andreas, a fellow architecture student at Illinois. A Richard Williams was a professor in the School of Architecture from 1946 to 1970, and served as long-time director of the graduate design studio. In his memoir, Williams lists Woods as a contributor to several of his projects.[9]

In the same year (1959) that Heinz von Foerster launched the Biological Computer Laboratory, the University of Illinois instituted the Center for Advanced Study, a campus-wide hub for faculty and visiting scholars to connect, pursue research and share their work. By 1967 the Center needed bespoke facilities. Williams renovated the interior of a large house near the eastern end of the campus to serve as its headquarters. He provided meeting rooms, dining and reception areas, and faculty and administrative offices, 'stimulating a renaissance of interdisciplinary activity'.[10]

In a letter to Williams that Woods probably wrote in 1970, he reflected: 'As we were sitting in the Center last night ... my attention was turned to our immediate environment, the lounge in which we sat and talked of such weighty things. I must say that your remodelling of that old house is marvellous – it is warm, direct and unpretentious, touched with your own compassion and humanity. It is absolutely appropriate for what I, at least, understand as the catalytic function of the Center itself.'[11]

The Center hosted a stimulating mix of on- and off-campus scholars from the humanities, arts and sciences who held both junior- and senior-level appointments. Williams himself was appointed an associate in 1967/68 to finalise the 'Century for Design: Countermeasure to the Urban Crisis' exhibition for the Krannert Art Museum. Experimental composer John Cage was in residence with Williams at this time, returning in 1968/69 when he was joined by the Chilean biologist and philosopher, and von Foerster's colleague, Humberto Maturana. Woods remembered this context in his description of the von Foerster household: '[T]here were all kinds of academics passing from Europe through the University, which, especially at that time, was a major university in Computer Science, in Physics, Mathematics, Music, and all the rest. So, they had this kind of soiree, and I was just this young guy kind of saying, "Oh, this is pretty amazing".'[12]

In 1969, Williams published a lengthy essay in a faculty newspaper called *The Laputa Gazette*. He wrote: 'The architect ... is a total theatre designer embracing an almost infinite variety of audience-actor relationships, stages and linkages between them.'[13] While Williams retired from the University of Illinois Urbana-Champaign in 1970,

Lebbeus Woods,
Drawing from *Architecture-Sculpture-Painting*,
1979

Initially included in Woods's self-publication *Architecture-Sculpture-Painting*, this drawing was later republished in A Richard Williams's book *The Urban Stage* (1980). As rendered by Woods, the 'stage' is prepared for the 'actors' to enter, but their vectorial energies are already fully present.

Lebbeus Woods,
Cover image for *Matrix: The Red Herring Poets*,
1976

below left: In 1976, poet Robert Bensen, the editor of the *Matrix* chapbook, invited his friend Woods to provide images for inclusion with poems by 18 Red Herring Poets, a local poetry collective. Woods's black-and-white cover recalls a bird's-eye view of gridded agricultural land, a familiar pattern of Midwestern large-scale agriculture. In the mid-1970s, University of Illinois architecture professor Bruce Hutchings provided Woods his first-ever flight over Urbana in his small plane, allowing Woods this view from the sky.

Lebbeus Woods,
Untitled drawing for *Matrix: The Red Herring Poets*,
1976

below right: A helmeted figure in profile is one of the inside images for *Matrix*. Woods's drawings stand alone; they do not illustrate the poems. Rendered in ink and preserved in the Lebbeus Woods Archive, this image is part of Woods's 'Journey Obelisk Wind' series of eight drawings.

he continued to develop these ideas. In 1980 he wrote in *The Urban Stage*: 'URBAN STAGE [is] a metaphor reflecting my growing feeling that as architects and urban planners we are set designers for real-life drama at all levels of private and public life.'[14] His interest in 'stages and linkages' echoed other theorists, specifically citing the performance scholar Richard Schechner's book *Environmental Theater* (1973).[15] Woods's own remarks on environmental theatre and its potentials are interspersed throughout his Notebooks of that time, showing fascination with similar themes.

Dreaming and Form-giving

Poet Robert Bensen, who first met Woods in Champaign in 1973, described him as a man of 'titanic energies' and 'volcanic' imagination.[16] 'Performing Leb' (as Bensen called it) included dragging fingers through his thick hair, drawing ceaselessly, fuelled by cigarettes and Coca-Cola, and listening to Richard Wagner's operas at high volume. Woods named the studio he occupied in 1975 in downtown Champaign the 'dream museum'. In turn, Bensen published 'In the Dream Museum', his poem describing Woods's imaginative process.[17] Bensen was also the editor of a chapbook, *Matrix*, featuring the local collective Red Herring Poets. For the inaugural *Matrix*, Woods provided five black-and-white drawings to accompany the poems.

In 'Notes on the World Myth', Woods declared: 'Artists and architects ... are cast as the form givers of the greatest mass ritual in history and must join the high priests of that drama or retire forever from the field.'[18] He aimed to instantiate this drama in his work. In a 1998 interview, he said: 'If you're doing work, on a certain level, it's always autobiographical – certainly in my case, kind of itinerant and, in a way, rootless in terms of a particular place.'[19] Woods's itinerant young adulthood brought him back to New York City. He continued to invent worlds; none was keyed to a physical address, whether in Manhattan or the Midwest.[20] ⌂

Notes
1. Lebbeus Woods, 'Terra Nova', in Peter Noever (ed), *Architecture in Transition: Between Deconstruction and New Modernism*, Prestel (Munich), 1991, p 134.
2. Lebbeus Woods, 'Notes on the World Myth', typescript, 1970, A Richard Williams Papers, 12/2/30, Box 2, General Correspondence, 1961–83, University of Illinois Archives.
3. A Richard Williams, *The Urban Stage: A Reflexion of Architecture and Urban Design,* San Francisco Center for Architecture and Urban Studies (San Francisco, CA), 1980.
4. Lebbeus Woods, 'Origins', 2 January 2012: https://lebbeuswoods.wordpress.com/2012/01/02/origins/; Lebbeus Woods, 'The Experimental', 12 August 2010: https://lebbeuswoods.wordpress.com/2010/08/12/the-experimental/.
5. Betty J Blum, 'Oral History of Ambrose M. Richardson' [1990], Chicago Architects Oral History Project, Department of Architecture, The Art Institute of Chicago, 2005, p 168.
6. Lebbeus Woods, 'Assembly Hall: pro, con', *The Daily Illini*, 17 March 1964, col 3, p 7.
7. 'Award Prizes in Architecture', *The Daily Illini*, 11 February 1961, col 1, p 2.
8. Lebbeus Woods, 'Junk', 1 June 2008: https://lebbeuswoods.wordpress.com/2008/06/01/junk/.
9. A Richard Williams, *Archipelago: Critiques of Contemporary Architecture and Education*, Osimo Press (Champaign, IL), 2009, pp 193–4.
10. *Ibid*, p 160.
11. Lebbeus Woods to A Richard Williams, 19 November 1970 (?), A Richard Williams Papers, 12/2/30, Box 2, General Correspondence, 1961–83, University of Illinois Archives.
12. *Lebbeus Woods is an Archetype*, SCI-Arc Press (Los Angeles), 2013, p 113.
13. A Richard Williams, 'Aries Ascending: Campus Architecture', *The Laputa Gazette,* 1 (5), 15 February 1969, p 7: https://digital.library.illinois.edu/items/5c12fbe0-f2ca-0138-7414-02d0d7bfd6e4-2.
14. A Richard Williams, *The Urban Stage, op cit*, p xi, n 3.
15. Richard Schechner, *Environmental Theater*, Hawthorn Books (New York), 1973.
16. Author Zoom interview with Robert Bensen, 19 August 2022.
17. Robert Bensen, 'In the Dream Museum', *Matrix II: The Red Herring Poets*, April 1977.
18. Lebbeus Woods, 'Notes on the World Myth', *op. cit*, n 2.
19. *Lebbeus Woods is an Archetype, op cit*, p 111.
20. I would like to thank the staff at the University of Illinois Archives, Charles Albanese (Executor of A Richard Williams' estate), Robert Bensen, Bruce Hutchings, Tait Johnson, Jeffrey Poss and Andreas von Foerster for their valuable help in preparing this essay.

The Dream Museum,
Champaign, Illinois,
1975

Photograph by Lebbeus Woods of the studio space at 205½ North Market Street, the address he recorded in his Black Noteboook #18, 25 October 1975 – 14 January 1976.

Text © 2024 John Wiley & Sons Ltd. Images: pp 22, 26–9 © The Estate of Lebbeus Woods; pp 24–5 Courtesy of the University of Illinois at Urbana-Champaign Archives, image 0006887.

Ben Sweeting

FROM EXPERIMENTAL EPISTEMOLOGY TO EXPERIMENTAL ARCHITECTURE

Frontispiece to a copy of 'The Need of Perception for the Perception of Needs' (1975) sent by Heinz von Foerster to Lebbeus Woods in November 1984

'The Need of Perception for the Perception of Needs' was a keynote address to the 1975 Convention of the American Institute of Architects (AIA), one of several instances in which von Foerster engaged with architecture and design. A connection with architecture ran through several generations of the von Foerster family: Heinz's son Andreas von Foerster, grandfather Emil von Förster (1838–1909) and great-grandfather Ludwig von Förster (1797–1863) were all architects.

A life-long beacon for Lebbeus Woods was his understanding of the ideas of second-order cybernetics and attempts to assimilate them into his architectural projects. An introduction to this discourse was provided in Urbana-Champaign in the early 1960s by his most important intellectual mentor, cyberneticist Heinz von Foerster. Poised at the intersection of architecture and cybernetics, **Ben Sweeting** charts some of the lines of their interactions and friendship.

During their time studying architecture at the University of Illinois Urbana-Champaign in the early 1960s, Lebbeus Woods and fellow student Andreas von Foerster set up a studio in the basement of the von Foerster family home. The hospitality of Andreas's parents, Heinz and Mai, which included 'coffee and tidbits even at four o'clock in the morning',[1] led to a deep connection that was sustained over subsequent decades.

Heinz von Foerster (1911–2002) was founder and director of the Biological Computer Laboratory (BCL) at Urbana-Champaign, an unusual research centre that was key to developments in the equally unusual field of cybernetics from the late 1950s until the laboratory's closure in the mid-1970s. Through von Foerster, Woods encountered topics that went well beyond the usual range of architectural discourse, while also being introduced to new contexts: the von Foersters were the first Europeans Woods had known.

Heinz von Foerster was prominent in the development of cybernetics and a pivotal figure in the reflexive turn of second-order cybernetics from the 1970s. Finding few opportunities to pursue a career as a scientist in postwar Europe, he had emigrated to the US in February 1949. Shortly after his arrival, he gained the attention of neurophysiologist Warren McCulloch, who was then on the faculty of the University of Illinois Chicago. McCulloch was chair of the Macy conferences and von Foerster attended from the 6th conference (March 1949), becoming one of the editors of the proceedings. McCulloch's support was instrumental in von Foerster gaining a position at the University of Illinois Urbana-Champaign, initially in the electron tube laboratory.

Woods provided illustrations for von Foerster's papers, gradually absorbing their ideas. The illustrations included a series of drawings of neural networks that featured in von Foerster's 1967 paper 'Computation in Neural Nets',[2] some of which were later reused by von Foerster in 'On Constructing a Reality' (1973), a recurring point of reference for Woods over subsequent decades.[3] Their relationship is documented in published comments by Woods and correspondence in Woods's archive, as well as in archival holdings at the University of Illinois and the University of Vienna. Some of this material has been the subject of research by Daryl McCurdy[4] and Dulmini Perera on whose work I build here.[5]

Constructing Realities
Von Foerster's work at the BCL continued McCulloch's 'experimental epistemology' research programme – an approach to understanding the mind in terms of the biological processes in which it is embodied, rather than through idealised rational models. While the main influence of 'On Constructing a Reality' has been in extensions of this epistemological tradition, its ideas were originally presented as an invited address to the Fourth International Environmental Design Research Association Conference held at the Virginia Polytechnic Institute (now Virginia Tech) in 1973.

Woods's illustrations for 'On Constructing a Reality' play an important part in von Foerster's arguments about cognition, ethics and aesthetics. Von Foerster describes how simple organisms have independent sensorimotor units distributed over their surfaces. These translate sensation directly into action,

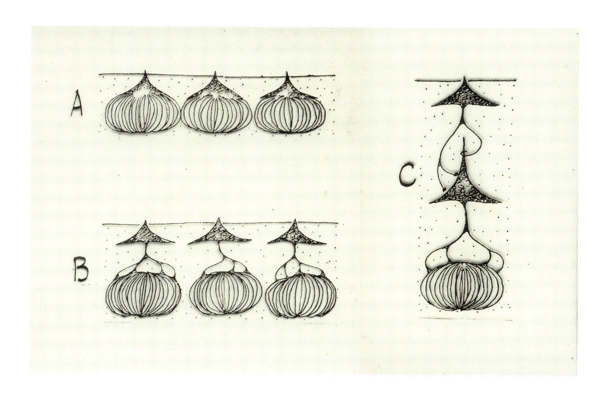

Lebbeus Woods,
Primitive nerve nets,
published in Heinz von Foerster,
'Computation in Neural Nets',
1967 and republished (with
minor modification) in 'On
Constructing a Reality',
1973

above: Woods provided illustrations for von Foerster's papers, such as this depiction of the evolution of the intermediate neuron (labelled C), which was crucial in the development of the mammalian nervous system.

Lebbeus Woods,
*Arrival of fibres at the
target layer of an action
network of cell assemblies*,
published in Heinz von Foerster,
'Computation in Neural Nets',
1967

right: 'Computation in Neural Nets' built on the work of von Foerster's own mentor, Warren McCulloch, who had shown that neural networks such as those Woods illustrated behave heterarchically not hierarchically. The concept of heterarchy was later invoked by Woods in a number of projects, most explicitly *Heterarchies* (1990).

Heinz von Foerster at the
door of the Biological Computer
Laboratory (BCL) office,
University of Illinois
Urbana-Champaign,
c 1967

opposite: The BCL was a leading international hub for research in cybernetics from the late 1950s to the mid-1970s, focusing on topics such as bionics and self-organising systems.

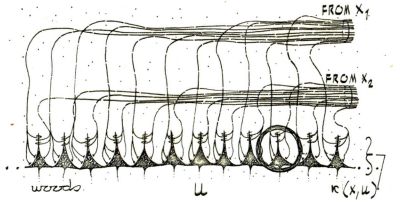

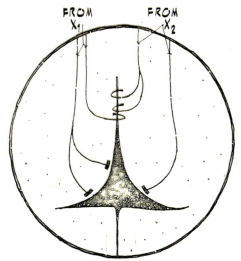

Letter from Lebbeus Woods
to Heinz von Foerster,
29 July 1986

The idea for the book project 'Cycles of Unity' exists only as a mock-up. It was most likely transformed into *OneFiveFour* (1989), which Woods dedicated to von Foerster.

> = copy
>
> 29 July 1986
>
> Dear Heinz,
>
> Thank you for sending <u>Observing Systems</u> and your paper "Order-Disorder." Coupled with the <u>Cybernetics of Cybernetics</u> book, they have already given my book composing efforts substantial impetus. Yours and Mai's visit was not only extremely enjoyable, but fortuitous with regard to my attempts to clarify my thoughts and experimental projects of the past thirteen years. I am calling the book presenting this body of work <u>Cycles of Unity</u>. I am learning much from the books, as I have always learned in my contacts with you, fleeting as they may have been, since the early 60's. In fact, our recent dialogue served to remind me just how profound an influence you have been in my life, in terms of my work and the thoughts with which I approach it. Rather selfishly, I hope that we can increase our dialogue in the future.
>
> Enclosed are four diagrams for my book, with indicative captions. I borrowed the picture of the brain from <u>Cybernetics of Cybernetics</u>, which I hope meets with your approval. I would like to illustrate a future paper of yours, if you would like it.
>
> We would like to come and visit you in the early autumn—is there a particular time that would suit you?
>
> Our love to you and Mai,

Postcard from Lebbeus Woods
to Heinz and Mai von Foerster,
1988

A record of a visit to the Pescadero home of Heinz and Mai von Foerster, while Woods's *Underground Berlin* project was being exhibited in San Francisco.

such as changes in shape, which in turn may lead to changes in sensation. The evolution of central nervous systems was enabled by the introduction of intermediate neurons, mediating between sensing and acting by processing how to respond and changing subsequent ways of responding. This development allowed more complex structures to evolve, where vast networks of neurons form internal connections through which they act on each other. With these internal connections, it is not just sensation that is processed; the nervous system also recursively processes the processes themselves.

In the human brain, the number of internal sensitivities significantly exceeds the number of external ones. As von Foerster outlines, what are taken to be qualities of external environments are the result of recursive processes internal to cognition: '"Out there" there is no light and no color, there are only electromagnetic waves; "out there" there is no sound and no music, there are only periodic variations of the air pressure; "out there" there is no heat and no cold, there are only moving molecules with more or less mean kinetic energy, and so on. Finally, for sure, "out there" there is no pain.'[6] Von Foerster is not denying the realities of light, sound, heat and pain, but repositioning where these realities are understood to lie. This complicates conventional assumptions about the relationship between environments and their inhabitants, with relationships between external and internal worlds becoming understood in terms of adaptation rather than reaction.

Von Foerster's repositioning of the qualities of environments as internal to cognition challenges the idea of environmental design. What does it mean to design an environment if the qualities of environments are internal to cognition? Conventionally, what architects are understood to be designing is 'the' environment. But, understanding environments as internal to cognition, there are not one but multiple environments within any situation created by parallel cognitive processes, hence constructing 'a' rather than 'the' reality. What architects are doing, then, is not designing 'the' environment but, rather, designing the constraints and affordances within which multiple possible environments can come to exist.

For von Foerster, this is also an ethical issue. Autonomy is a fundamental part of all cognition, not only of conscious decision-making. Given this, he characterises objectivity as a nonsensical attempt to exclude the properties of observers from the descriptions of their observations – an exclusion that is ethically flawed in its obfuscation of individual autonomy and responsibility. Woods's projects and writing relate this ethical stance to the ways in which architectural spaces are inhabited and designed.

Ethical and Aesthetical Imperatives
'On Constructing a Reality' closes with two imperatives: '*The ethical imperative*: Act always so as to increase the number of choices' and '*The aesthetical imperative*: If you desire to see, learn how to act.'[7] Both are rooted in von Foerster's discussion of cognition and criticism of objectivity. Perception is not the passive reception of information, but dependent on and coordinated through action. One cannot explain (excuse) actions as consequences of the external environment because the environment is not external. Individuals have autonomy over their actions and perceptions and therefore choices to make about how they act and perceive, choices that are often obfuscated through objectivity.

Von Foerster often associated both imperatives with dialogue and the connotative function of language, contrasting them with the monological and denotive character of objective description. Addressing the 1975 Convention of the American Institute of Architects (AIA) in Atlanta, Georgia, von Foerster connected the ethical imperative to architecture by understanding architectural spaces in dialogical and connotative terms: 'The language of Architecture is essentially connotative, for its intent is to initiate interpretation: the creative architectural space begets creativity, new insights, new choices. It is a catalyst for cognitions.'[8]

While some architectural spaces do invite new possibilities in the way von Foerster describes, many do not. The conventional built environment is often monological and denotive. Conventional architectural typologies, programmes and spaces constrain the possible realities they afford. Monumental architecture codifies dominant understandings, which then come to seem inevitable. Even the use of language as a way of thinking about architecture has often been in a denotative, representational sense.

Woods explicitly related the ethical and aesthetical imperatives to the architectural spaces of *Underground Berlin* (1988) – his project for 'a city beneath a city' with a network of structures that act as living laboratories 'in which living is experimental and in which the ongoing experiment is living'.[9] In contrast to the monological character of the conventional built environment, the spatial configurations of Woods's *Underground Berlin* require invention, imagination and resourcefulness from their occupants. It is an architecture that invites acting in order to perceive, and that requires an increasing number of choices to be made – an architecture for constructing 'a' rather than 'the' reality.

Continued Dialogue
The dialogue between Woods and von Foerster continued beyond their shared time at Urbana-Champaign. Woods credited von Foerster with giving impetus to the development of *OneFiveFour* (1989), a book project initially conceived under the title 'Cycles of Unity'.[10] Two of the drawings for 'Cycles of Unity' were inspired by illustrations of the brain featured in the 1974 'Cybernetics of Cybernetics' publication that had been developed by von Foerster and students at the BCL.[11] These drawings were concerned with the same processes of cognition as Woods's neural network illustrations, but now envisioned in experiential and architectural terms.

While the influence of von Foerster on Woods was considerable, it was not a linear translation of ideas. In line with the above understanding of autonomy and responsibility, Woods's development of von Foerster's ideas was not limited to von Foerster's intentions: 'It's very important to him [Heinz von Foerster] that each individual develop their own interpretation of ideas, their own way of seeing things … I knew there were certainly things he didn't agree with or that I had interpreted it differently than maybe he'd intended, but he respected my right to interpret these ideas in the way that I do.'[12]

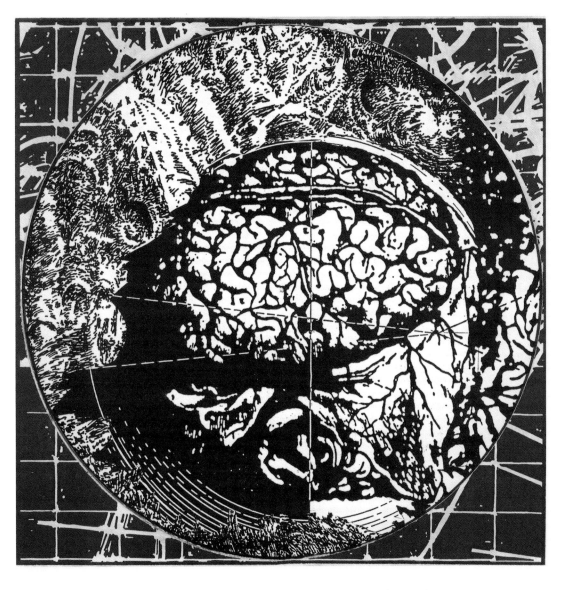

Lebbeus Woods,
Electromagnetic turbulence: thought/form distinction,
'Cycles of Unity',
c 1985

In preparing the 'Cycles of Unity' book project, Woods borrowed two images of the brain from the 1974 'Cybernetics of Cybernetics' publication produced by Heinz von Foerster and students at the Biological Computer Laboratory (BCL). The original illustrations are the work of 16th-century anatomist Andreas Vesalius.

The relationship between Lebbeus Woods and Heinz von Foerster was founded on shared epistemological and ethical foundations that spanned very different fields

Lebbeus Woods,
Quadrapolar distortions: violation of the second law, 'Cycles of Unity', c 1985

In this drawing, Woods envisions the mind in architectural and experiential terms, complementing the earlier neurophysiological illustrations he completed for Heinz von Foerster. The composition resonates deeply with the agenda of von Foerster's second-order cybernetics, which called for the observation of observation, in contrast to the conventional exclusion of the scientific observer.

Exploring the relations between autonomy, cognition, ethics and aesthetics in the social and material situation of designing architecture, Woods's interpretations go beyond the abstract notion of the observer that characterises von Foerster's work. When an adaptation of von Foerster's 1975 AIA address was published in the journal *Leonardo*,[13] Woods supplied a commentary on it,[14] to which von Foerster in turn responded.[15] In this exchange, Woods clarifies the role of the dialogical in von Foerster's argument by situating it in terms of the social relations within which architecture is designed. Woods differentiates dialogue from standard forms of consultation, instead characterising it as a sensibility in the practice of architecture that recognises the need for freedom from coercion by the architect, client and the architecture itself. To achieve this, Woods argues, it is necessary for architects themselves to act with autonomy. Replicating the ideas and tastes of clients, public institutions and popular culture will lead to environments that in turn demand conformity from those who inhabit them.

The relationship between Lebbeus Woods and Heinz von Foerster was founded on shared epistemological and ethical foundations that spanned very different fields. While the illustrations of neural networks seem removed from the topic of architecture, there is a continuity of ideas running between these drawings and Woods's architectural work over the following decades. Woods might therefore be characterised as not simply influenced by the experimental epistemology of von Foerster and McCulloch, but as significantly extending this tradition into the context of architecture.[16] ⌁

Notes
1. Heinz von Foerster, 'John Simon Guggenheim Memorial Foundation: Confidential Report on Candidate for Fellowship', Box 12, Heinz von Foerster Papers, Illinois University Library: https://digital.library.illinois.edu/items/d04f40a0-f54f-0134-23e3-0050569601ca-f
2. Heinz von Foerster, *Understanding Understanding: Essays on Cybernetics and Cognition*, Springer-Verlag (New York), 2003, ch 2.
3. Ibid, ch 8.
4. Daryl McCurdy, 'Lebbeus Woods, Architect', 9 May 2013: https://openspace.sfmoma.org/2013/05/lw-daryl-mccurdy/.
5. Dulmini Perera, 'Architectures of Coevolution: Second-order Cybernetics and Architectural Theories of the Environment, c. 1959–2013', Doctoral thesis, University of Hong Kong, 2017: https://repository.hku.hk/handle/10722/249220.
6. Heinz von Foerster, *Understanding Understanding*, op cit, p 216.
7. Ibid, p 227.
8. Heinz von Foerster, 'The Need of Perception for the Perception of Needs', BCL Report no 13.3, 1975, p. 16. Adaptation of keynote address to the 1975 Convention of the American Institute of Architects, Illinois University Library: https://digital.library.illinois.edu/items/26e627b0-2c83-0136-4d81-0050569601ca-c.
9. Lebbeus Woods, *OneFiveFour*, Princeton Architectural Press (New York), 1989, pp 4 and 6.
10. Ibid.
11. 'Cybernetics of Cybernetics: Or the Control of Control and the Communication of Communication', BCL Report no 73.38, Illinois University Library: https://digital.library.illinois.edu/items/2504bc20-2c83-0136-4d81-0050569601ca-5.
12. *Lebbeus Woods is an Archetype*, SCI-Arc Press (Los Angeles, CA), 2013, pp 113–14.
13. Heinz von Foerster, 'The Need of Perception for the Perception of Needs', *Leonardo*, 22 (2), 1989, pp 223–6.
14. Lebbeus Woods, 'Commentary on "Need of Perception for the Perception of Needs"', *Leonardo*, 23 (1), 1990, pp 157–8.
15. Heinz von Foerster, 'Response to Lebbeus Woods's Comment', *Leonardo*, 23 (1), 1990, p 158.
16. Thanks to: Bethany Anderson and the University of Illinois Archives; Marcus J Carney, Marianne Ertl, and The Heinz von Foerster, Gordon Pask & Cybernetics Archives at the Department of Contemporary History, University of Vienna; Andreas von Foerster; Sharon Irish; Dulmini Perera; Paul Schroeder; Tanya Southcott; Neil Spiller; Sally Sutherland; and Aleksandra Wagner.

Text © 2024 John Wiley & Sons Ltd. Images: pp 30, 34(t), 36–7 © The Estate of Lebbeus Woods; p 32 Courtesy of the University of Illinois at Urbana-Champaign Archives; pp 33(t&b), 34(b) © The Heinz von Foerster, Gordon Pask & Cybernetics Archives (University of Vienna)

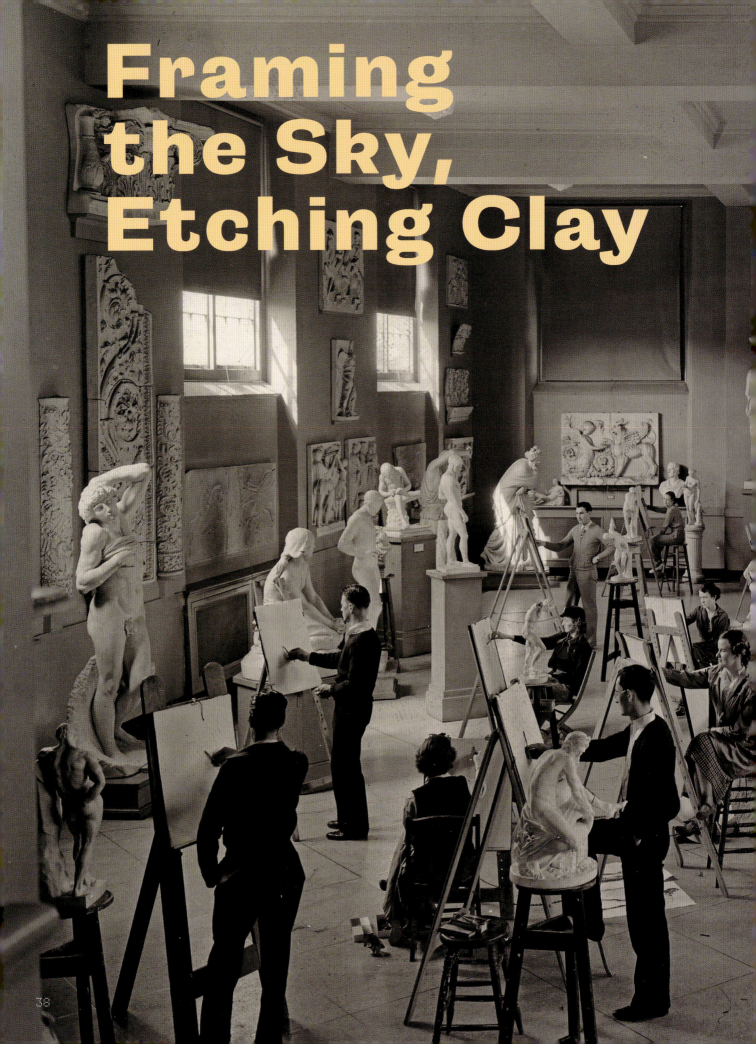

Framing the Sky, Etching Clay

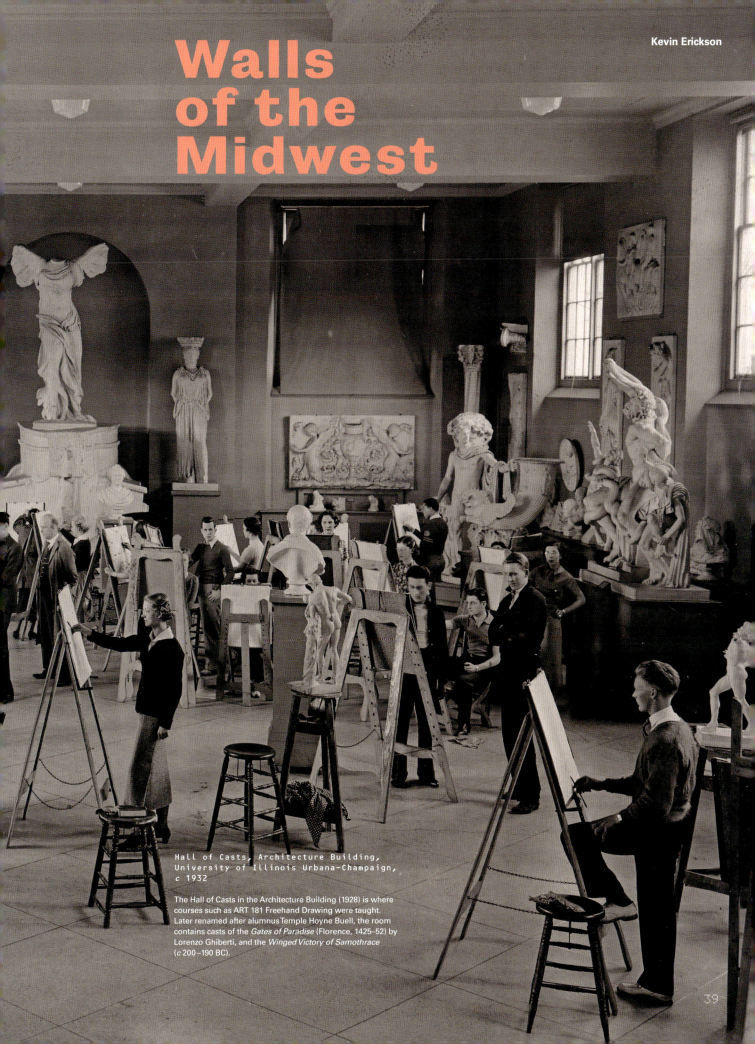

Walls of the Midwest

Kevin Erickson

Hall of Casts, Architecture Building,
University of Illinois Urbana-Champaign,
c 1932

The Hall of Casts in the Architecture Building (1928) is where courses such as ART 181 Freehand Drawing were taught. Later renamed after alumnus Temple Hoyne Buell, the room contains casts of the *Gates of Paradise* (Florence, 1425–52) by Lorenzo Ghiberti, and the *Winged Victory of Samothrace* (c 200–190 BC).

The American Midwest with its own architectural histories and topologies may be termed a land of few walls. Architect **Kevin Erickson** examines Lebbeus Woods's relation to this landscape and the genesis of his preoccupation with walls, not as protectors of boundaries, but as sites of dialogue and collaboration. Rather than mere surfaces for large paintings, walls – new or abandoned – invite reflection on the relationship between art and architecture.

What would one expect to find looking over the slides in the Lebbeus Woods Archive? A record of the work, of course. Sometimes labelled, most often not; sometimes easily recognisable, often not recognisable at all – certainly not to those unfamiliar with the beginnings of his career.

It is not only a career one would have to be familiar with in order to discern the content of his Midwest visual library. It is the landscape – lived and historical – that informed his ideas.

A Heartland

The Midwest, often referred to as the Heartland for its centralist values, is a flat plain spanning two mountain ranges formed by glaciers which left a rich layer of topsoil and mineral deposits. Its geography and abundant natural resources have allowed the region to develop as the US's most significant producer of agricultural and industrial products.

Organised by Thomas Jefferson's notion of a grid, the Land Ordinance of 1785 is perhaps one of the largest planning or land division experiments ever. Structured on principal meridian and base lines, tiers and ranges were established with one 6-by-6-mile (10-by-10-kilometre) square forming a township that is divided further. The grid is a dominant feature of the Midwest, one of the reasons why this vast and sparsely populated space lacks a singular identity.

Large metropolitan areas of Chicago and Detroit influenced most of the architectural landscape, the development of infrastructure and, with it, the sky-reaching ambitions. The Great Chicago Fire of 1871 was a defining point. In 1884, William Le Baron Jenney created the first steel-frame structure – the Home Insurance Building, Chicago. The Sears Tower (now Willis Tower), by Skidmore, Owings & Merrill, stood as the world's tallest building for nearly a quarter of a century after its completion in 1974, only to be bested by the Petronas Towers in Kuala Lumpur (1997), the work of University of Illinois Urbana-Champaign alumnus César Pelli. In the years around 1900, while Chicago was developing up, Frank Lloyd Wright was building out. One of the best examples of his early Prairie style is the Dana-Thomas House (1904) in Springfield, Illinois. In Detroit, Albert Kahn was working with Henry Ford on the Highland Park Ford Plant (1909), the origin of the assembly line.

In between two World Wars, Eliel Saarinen and Mies van der Rohe landed in the Midwest. Soon after being recognised for his Tribune Tower competition entry (1922), Saarinen embarked on the work for the Cranbrook campus in Bloomfield Hills, Michigan, where he headed its Department of Architecture and Urban Design from 1932 to 1950. Mies arrived in 1938 to what is now the Illinois Institute of Technology (IIT), and directed the Department of Architecture until 1958. The two private institutions were arguably the centre of American architectural discourse during that period.

Kevin Erickson,
Agrarian winter landscape,
2016

After the harvest and before the beginning of July, the Midwest's terrain is visible for a country mile.

Kevin Erickson,
Midwest of 1975,
2023

The space between the Mississippi and Ohio Rivers and Lake Michigan, with the University of Illinois at its centre. Depicted are works of architecture reachable by car.

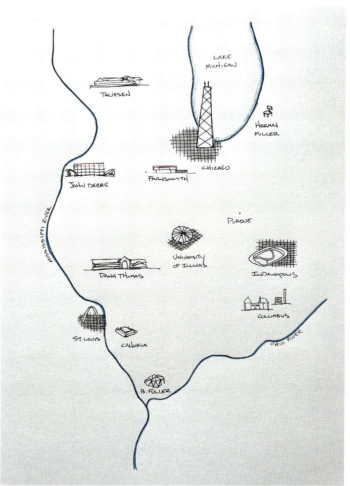

An Island

Surrounded by corn and soya beans for over a hundred miles (160 kilometres) in every direction, Urbana-Champaign is an island with one of the oldest schools of architecture in the US – at the University of Illinois Urbana-Champaign (founded 1867). In 1873 it was the first to graduate a student from an architecture programme: Nathan Ricker. Lebbeus Woods attended the school from 1960 to 1964 during one of the most significant periods in its history.

At that time, another alumnus, Max Abramovitz, was landing a spaceship on campus in the form of Assembly Hall (1963); in the same context, he would later complete the Krannert Center for the Performing Arts (1969). Paul Rudolph was commissioned for the Christian Science Student Center (1965; razed in 1986). Faculty member A Richard 'Dick' Williams designed the Education Building (1964), which sits directly in front of the Architecture Building. Every student working in the second- and third-floor studios would have had a front-row seat to its construction.

While these examples point to an institutional investment in a high level of architectural production, equally important work was being accomplished through single-family residential projects. Dick Williams termed his own style as 'Mid-Continent Modernism', a balanced mix of Minimalist simplicity, functional pragmatism and environmental harmony.[1] Other faculty members such as Jack Baker and John Replinger were experimenting with their own versions of High Modernism; Bruce Goff completed a speculative house (Garvey House No 1, 1954) for violinist and School of Music faculty member John Garvey and his wife, also a musician.

Lebbeus Woods left this scene at its high point. When he returned in 1967 – shortly before the US's escalation in the Vietnam War – the whole country, not only Urbana-Champaign, was a different place.

Everyday Architecture

Most of the Midwest's built fabric is not of high design: it mirrors the repetitive sameness of its gridded organisation. Aside from a church, library or civic building, the majority of everyday architecture is rather banal. It has grown even more so with suburban sprawl and corporate ownership far removed from and blind to the context. To some, this vast open space interrupted only by repetitive markers could be overwhelming and anxiety provoking; to others, the known repetition was a source of comfort; to yet others, it provided boundless possibilities.

How does one practise architecture when positioned between the vastness of nature and the repetitiveness of commercial culture? Or, as Woods put it in one of his early notebooks, how to find an adequate expression – identify the form – amongst 'the nondescript prairie, the scattered houses, the roads, the overwhelming sky?'[2]

One way to reflect on this question is by focusing on two of his own projects – both involving cementitious walls, each heavy with a different meaning.

As one would expect, Woods had to be involved in commercial work. As one would expect, too, this type of work was of no interest to him: 'I am not interested in designing buildings and objects for people, institutions and causes that I am not only indifferent to, but in many cases I am vehemently opposed to … I might design a building someday, but it will be the sort of building that is only occasionally needed in society, a building that is the solitary statement of an artist and that serves almost solely as a vehicle for that statement.'[3] Nevertheless, he took on a quintessential piece of everyday architecture: the wall.

Walls

While director of design at Integrative Design Solutions (IDS) in Champaign between 1972 and 1975, Woods was working on a shopping centre and suburban housing development at Lake of the Woods, 10 miles (16 kilometres) northwest of Champaign. The first portion to be executed was a bar and liquor store (1972–4). His response to the brief was somewhere between a decorated shed and a deconstructed box with a triangular footprint.

Built with a commonplace assembly of concrete masonry perimeter walls and a lightweight steel-supported flat roof, the exterior is taken a step further, clad entirely with vertical wood siding and punctured with a variety of cut-outs on all elevations. Furthermore, the façade is elaborated with enlarged colourful images projecting the commercial intent.

However, the entry sequence is where the thesis lies. The 'billboard' façade directs patrons through two large punctures on opposing ends into triangular voids, partially enclosed, partially exposed. Suspended between the parking lot and the prairie, this elongated poche is rendered with a vibrant red. The varying geometric shapes reveal a framed sky and landscape beyond.

Like other American cities in 1975, Downtown Champaign was experiencing a decline. The City considered several urban revitalisation strategies and ultimately converted its main thoroughfare into a covered pedestrian mall. To mark the nation's coming bicentenary in 1976, the City sought artwork to adorn public spaces adjacent to the mall. Woods submitted a proposal for a variety of locations and was selected for a site a few blocks away from his then new studio at 205½ North Market Street.

Lebbeus Woods,
Lake of the Woods Bar & Liquors,
Illinois,
1974

opposite top: The vestibule: an acute viewpoint from the exterior frames an entry scene.

opposite right: This building was the first executed element of a broader scheme for the small rural locality of Lake of the Woods in Champaign County. Woods photographed its front façade and entry in colour, but images of the side/rear elevation, such as this one, are documented in black and white, capturing long shadows projecting on the prairie grassland.

Lebbeus Woods,
Odysseus in the Midwestern urban landscape,
1975

Etched on a wall of Chicago common brick, *Odysseus* seems to be echoing Woods's statement that 'figures, symbols, colors, lines and words adorn and challenge walls, threatening their severity, their heavy, puritan dignity with the highest human laughter' – Lebbeus Woods, undated manuscript, 1970s, Lebbeus Woods Archive.

'I created my Odysseus on the abandoned wall of a building in Champaign, Illinois. … This wall of infinite shadings, textures and coloring is a mythic dominion as mysterious and remote as the lands and seas traveled by the Odysseus of Homer and Kazantzakis. From a curiously demonic stain, I partly found and partly drew this image of the insatiable wanderer.'

Unlike the object attempting to locate itself amidst the prairie, this site was a palimpsest, an abandoned brick wall layered with time and history: built up, torn down, exposed and weathered. In considering his approach to the 'found' condition, Woods faced a dilemma: 'Is it enough to consider these structural surfaces as simply more frame and canvas, on which the artist creates a large easel painting? Or, is there a special relationship that must be created between art and architecture?'[4]

He rejected 'any blatantly "patriotic" or strictly bicentennial or historic themes […] limited in both aesthetic and social durability'.[5] Instead, having explored ideas framed by James Joyce in *Finnegans Wake* (1939) and *Ulysses* (1920), Woods turned to the poet Nikos Kazantzakis. This choice is articulated retrospectively: 'I created my Odysseus on the abandoned wall of a building in Champaign, Illinois, sometime toward the end of October 1975. This wall of infinite shadings, textures and coloring is a mythic dominion as mysterious and remote as the lands and seas traveled by the Odysseus of Homer and Kazantzakis. From a curiously demonic stain, I partly found and partly drew this image of the insatiable wanderer.'[6]

The 'insatiable wanderer' was etched on a wall of Chicago common brick – a rough and unrefined type of brick, made of clay from the Chicago River, which was originally intended for side and rear elevations. The clay is full of lime, iron and small stone particulates, causing patina in a range of colours depending on composition. On such a wall, below what was once a landing and behind what was once a stairway, remained a patch of plaster. Woods's *Odysseus* lurked from it. He stood nearly 7 feet (2.1 metres) tall – or 33 brick courses, counting from the photograph – larger than an average human figure, closer to a mythical one: slightly looking down on the passers-by.

It is nearly uncanny that Woods chose to unmemorialise the American Empire by turning to the Greeks. It is equally significant that precisely this wall, imbued with local history and embedded in the Midwestern urban landscape, is what he left behind as one of his final marks. Did he know that his departure from the Midwest was imminent?

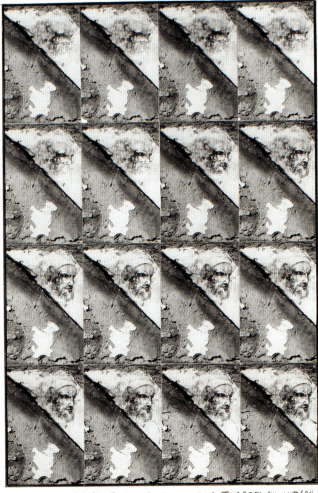

Lebbeus Woods,
Odysseus montage,
1977

above: Each stage of *Odysseus*'s construction was documented in situ. Woods's fascination with the technology of reproduction and its potentials is conveyed by this montage of images and the text, evoking 'the broad and endless experiental stream of which [each stage] is a mere portion'.

Lebbeus Woods,
Untitled,
1977

right: One of two untitled red drawings of walls from the *Odysseus* period: 'The walls remain, resisting, in their turn, the chaos of earth, but the mortal scrawls are changing' – Lebbeus Woods, undated manuscript, 1970s, Lebbeus Woods Archive.

The Ultimate Game

Woods revisited walls of the Midwest soon after arriving in New York in the spring of 1976. *Odysseus* was reconstructed as a discrete graphic work in a montage evocative of the motion studies of 19th-century photographer Eadweard Muybridge, and then in a self-published pamphlet with select images of the site at different scales.[7] In another pamphlet of the same year, he articulated his position regarding the intimate relationship between walls and drawings: 'The wall painted with images is more than a physical boundary, limiting and securing habitable space; it is a frontier between worlds of the real and the ideal, the material and the spiritual.'[8]

The Midwest, a land of few walls, was a formative beginning of Woods's thinking about walls – what they symbolise, project, screen, separate and enclose. This fascination with the vertical surface and its potentialities is consistently addressed in his later work.[9] *Underground Berlin* (1988), *Three Reconstructed Boxes* (1993), *War and Architecture: Walls* (1994), *Havana* (1995) – all trace their origins back to 1975 and to the statement: 'Architecture is the ultimate game of walls.'[10] ∆

Notes
1. A Richard Williams, Historical Note, University of Illinois Archives: https://archon.library.illinois.edu/archives/index.php?p=collections/controlcard&id=2895.
2. Lebbeus Woods, Black Notebook #8, 15 July – 25 September 1973 (entry of 21 July), unpaginated, Lebbeus Woods Archive.
3. Lebbeus Woods, Letter to IDS partners, 30 April 1973, Lebbeus Woods Archive.
4. Lebbeus Woods, Black Notebook #17, 6 May – 23 October 1975 (entry of 18 September), unpaginated, Lebbeus Woods Archive.
5. *Ibid.*
6. Lebbeus Woods, *Odysseus Wall Drawing*, Augustän-Xenon Press (New York), 1979, unpaginated.
7. *Ibid.*
8. Lebbeus Woods, *Painting: Toward the Heroic*, Augustän-Xenon Press (New York), 1979, pp 3–4.
9. Lebbeus Woods, 'The Wall Game', in Michael Sorkin (ed), *Against the Wall*, The New Press (New York), 2005, pp 260–65.
10. Woods, Black Notebook #17, entry of 20 May.

Text © 2024 John Wiley & Sons Ltd. Images: pp 38–9 Courtesy of the University of Illinois Archives, 0005127, R.S. 39/2/20, Box LMS-2, Folder LMS - 2 Architecture Building Gallery; p 41(t&b) © Kevin Erickson; pp 43(t&b), 45 Photos by Lebbeus Woods. © The Estate of Lebbeus Woods; pp 46–7 © The Estate of Lebbeus Woods

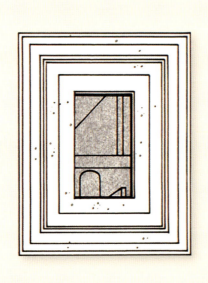

A POSTMO
EARLY SCENES OF SHO

BE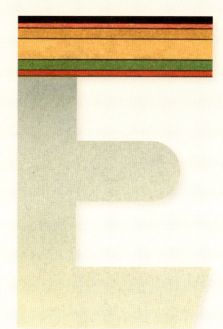SDERNiST?
PPiNG AND DWELLiNG

Aaron Betsky

Vivid colours, commedia dell'arte, collage and hypergraphics, and villae jutting out of the cliffsides designed for the unknown dwellers – are these projects postmodern? American art, architecture and design critic **Aaron Betsky** investigates this question and its context, focusing on the V.I.P. Center Shopping Mall, an unbuilt scheme that was to win Lebbeus Woods his first professional acknowledgement under the auspices of the Progressive Architecture Award.

After leaving the University of Illinois Urbana-Champaign, Lebbeus Woods laboured for a decade as an architect. Most notably, in 1964, he was employed by Roche Dinkeloo Associates, the successor firm to that founded by Eero Saarinen, whose work opened up Modernism to the more expressive and communicative forms that became key to Postmodernism. His main focus was on the Ford Foundation Building in New York City (1967), which is significant in itself because the structure's tumble of gardens descending in the midst of Manhattan's human-made ranges of skyscrapers could easily serve as a model for Woods's tectonic visions of buildings continually under construction. After this period, Woods's first stint in New York, he returned to the Midwest to work for the medium-sized firm Richardson, Severns, Scheeler & Associates from 1967 to 1970, before becoming director of design at Illinois Design Solutions (IDS) from 1972 to 1975.

Lebbeus Woods / Illinois Design Solutions (IDS),
The Ideal Square of a City,
The V.I.P. Center Shopping Mall proposal,
Indianapolis, Indiana,
1973

One aim of this unbuilt proposition was to invigorate the public realm. This drawing shows the mall as environmental theatre reminiscent of the ancient Greek agora, a gathering place, multivalent in its functions but dressed in a colourful postmodern coat of skins.

It was during his time at IDS that he won the Progressive Architecture Award (1974), for the research and development that went into the design of, of all things, a shopping mall. The P/A Awards, as they were known, were significant from the 1970s to the 1990s because they became the mechanism that many architects – from Michael Graves to Machado Silvetti, to name but two prominent examples – used to rise from obscurity or academia into, first, notoriety as avant-garde avatars of Postmodernism, and then leaders of that movement.

Playing with Allusions

The unbuilt proposal for the V.I.P. Center Shopping Mall, Indianapolis, Indiana (1972–3) is spectacular in both senses of that word. The set-up is fairly conventional: a meandering path cut through a single-storey block of shops, with the one twist that a block of apartments and a low-rise office structure were to be set on top of the mall. It is the manner in which Woods and IDS imagined the public space as 'an imaginary outdoor street of colorful shapes, lines, and patterns ... created with large scale wall graphics and storefronts which are offset from each other, creating an irregularity to the whole space'[1] that makes the proposal distinctive. The developers explained in their selling brochure (illustrated by Woods) that they were appealing to a 'young, medium to high income adult market'.[2]

Woods presented a series of collages of what appear to be columns, some of them freestanding, some of them part of what appear to be the shopfronts, surmounted by circles and abstracted pediments. These allusions to classical forms are so reduced, however, that they act more as organising geometries than as references. The numerous lines drawn over and through them, none of which seem to indicate any specific architecture or retail elements, cut through even that sense of solidity, as do the pastel-coloured lozenges, squares and chevrons Woods shows painted on the walls. Collaged figures wandering through this maze of fragments coexist with greyed-out portraits Woods lifted from Renaissance paintings. The vision does not recall any then-current shopping mall, instead evoking both the paintings of such Pop Art makers as Roy Lichtenstein, and the work of graphic designers such as Peter Max or April Greiman, and the kind of 'electronic expressionism' Robert Venturi and Denise Scott Brown had proposed as a result of their reading of Las Vegas.

Woods had immersed himself in the imagery, techniques and expressive aims of one aspect of the broad church of Postmodernism. It was the version of that movement that was interested in developing a stage-set version of architecture governed by fragmented grids that indicated the presence, but also a very modern breakdown of order; a rhythm of abstracted neoclassical elements that showed, in a purposefully eviscerated and playful manner, a desire for monumentality and meaning. Postmodernists who focused on these aspects of historical recall exhibited the results in combinations of perspective and collage that transformed these elements into a reality that could only be inhabited lightly and in fragments. Woods was working in that domain of architecture of which Charles Moore was the godfather. He also evoked the ways standard elements of architecture were enhanced and blown up by the likes of Stanley Tigerman, Arata Isozaki, Ettore Sottsass, Massimo Scolari, a young Eric Owen Moss and, especially, Frank Gehry. Gehry, who was then designing shopping malls and stores

Woods had immersed himself in the imagery, techniques and expressive aims of one aspect of the broad church of Postmodernism

Lebbeus Woods / Illinois Design Solutions (IDS),
Interior,
The V.I.P. Center Shopping Mall proposal,
Indianapolis, Indiana,
1973

The mall's architectural language is composed as a episodic sequence of set pieces that conspire to represent the building as a series of stage sets and possible exhibition/performative spaces.

Lebbeus Woods / Illinois Design Solutions (IDS),
Eat Street,
The V.I.P. Center Shopping Mall proposal,
Indianapolis, Indiana,
1973

Fashionable postmodern motifs of the day abound in this drawing. Strong colours, collage and hypergraphics, for example, all contribute to an architectural imperative to enliven the streetscape and make it fun. Yet this drawing has collaged within it a rotated text arguing that 'the Apollinian Age crust of the Earth is cracking. Nobility, balance, the sweetness of life, happiness, are all virtue[s] which we must have the courage to bid goodbye.'

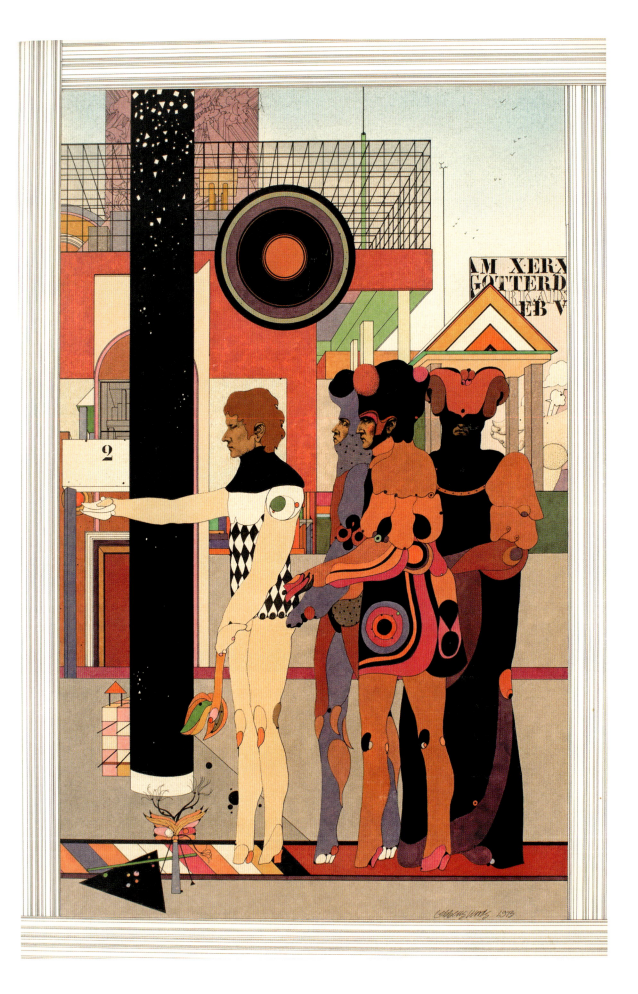

not unlike those Woods was imagining, is a particularly interesting parallel given how both his and Woods's work later developed.[3]

What Woods added to this form of Postmodernism were, quite specifically, the frenetic lines running through and over the somewhat familiar fragments of buildings – a mainstay of his later architecture. Here the lines sliced into parts of buildings, extended them, and sometimes ignored the integrity of form in favour of their own logic. 'L'effet c'est moi', Woods named one drawing he self-published in 1979.[4] Showing streets in an imaginary neighbourhood, the architecture recognises no single structure, instead creating a unified vision that evokes the backgrounds of Italian Renaissance paintings. Already the lines are tending towards an alternate geography. They are becoming vectors connecting buildings and describing spaces, as well as patterns that are completely taking over parts of the structures.

Beyond Home

The broader landscape Woods was beginning to excavate also shows up as the base for a design of HOUSE: Xn. (1979). The numbering recalls Peter Eisenman's sequential enumeration of his residential projects. The lack of finished interiors, or of any indication of what this project is as a complete structure, makes one realise that these are as much experiments in investigating the semantics of domestic inhabitations as they are proposals for dwellings. HOUSE: J. (1978) moves these explorations into a higher degree of abstraction; it leaves indications of walls, columns and floating planes to coexist with grids and lines that serve no apparent function, only to then present one interior view and one façade perspective suggesting incompleteness, without a clear border or edge, let alone function.

Villa Ä(--)X and Villae (U)R (both 1979) begin to reintroduce a more coherent context, albeit one that is extreme: cliffsides out of which the bits and pieces of the houses jut out, gathering themselves into vertically stacked elements that step back with the rise of the landscape and take their place among vegetation growing out of the rocks in a similar manner. Here the references seem to be to Chinese landscape painting, but, in the style of the drawings as well as their placements, they also recall Frank Lloyd Wright's Southern California projects as they were developed into houses by Rudolph Schindler and Richard Neutra in the 1920s and 1930s.

As the insides of these structures, we see vignettes of rooms looking back over the immediate – not the far – landscape. These spaces are cut apart by the relentless slicing of different levels, the presence of floating screens and unexplained, stepping objects that might be fireplaces or room dividers. All of these elements defy the Miesian tendency towards 'almost nothing', expressing more of a *horror vacui* than a desire to make a functional living space.

Lebbeus Woods /
Illinois Design Solutions (IDS),
Untitled,
The V.I.P. Center
Shopping Mall proposal,
Indianapolis, Indiana,
1973

opposite: People populate some of the drawings, providing a sense of anticipation, scale and expectation. Yet they too have allusions to past fashions, the *commedia dell'arte* and theatre costumes.

Lebbeus Woods,
HOUSE: Xn.,
1979

top: This interior one-point perspective depicts the main space of the house. It does not clearly declare itself or its function. The viewer is left unsure as to whether the enigmatic 'back wall' is a wall painting or a view through to another space.

Lebbeus Woods,
Villae (U)R,
1979

above: Woods's two house proposals were augmented in 1979 by two larger schemes for villas. Both occupy steeply inclined hillsides and mature wooded landscapes. Villae (U)R is monumental in scale, fractured and multilayered, providing opportunities for roof gardens, loggias and vistas punctuating its mass.

Beyond Scenes

To have a sense of how both the shopping mall project and the sketches of houses might extend into the larger realm that would draw out Woods's architecture, one can turn to 'City of Lines', a series of drawings that, judging by its placement in the Lebbeus Woods Archive, is nearly contemporaneous with the mall design.

Here the scenography extends into a version of an Italian Renaissance painting's depiction of the scene in which miracles might occur or saints might be martyred. In this case, however, there are no people present, and all indications of built form are again fractured, folded and layered together, and composed into strongly receding perspectives. In one of the drawings, stepped pyramids sprout gates and towers, evoking Giovanni Battista Piranesi's *Le Antichità Romane* (*The Antiquities of Rome*, 1756); in another, the amassing structures echo the fusing of geology and urban form of Antonio Sant'Elia's *Città Nuova* (*New City*, 1914).

Such historical references do not seem accidental. Woods made one of the 'City of Lines' drawings have the appearance of an etching, complete with hatched shading. It makes one consider the work of this period as a search for the pieces out of which he would subsequently construct his visionary experimental projects. The whole of architecture, but also art history, as well as the products of postmodern architects, were part of the scrapyard Woods scavenged for forms he then cleaned up, fragmented and abstracted.

What Woods seems to be searching for is a way to combine the highly abstract processes of involution and exploration, with the ability to evoke a sensual reality. Unwilling to step into the voids of pure geometry or semantics devolving into deconstruction, Lebbeus Woods draws perspectives that set scenes in which real people *could* imagine living.

Lebbeus Woods,
City of Lines,
early 1970s

This drawing distinguishes itself from the other four in this project in two ways. Firstly its use of cross-hatching to create shadow to further enhance its forms. Also it explores the interiority of the project whereas the other drawings are views of exterior streetscapes.

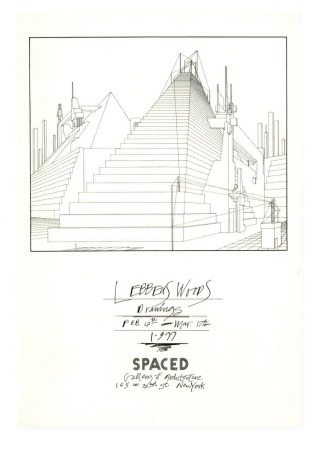

Lebbeus Woods,
Poster for the 'Spaced' exhibition,
1977

A drawing from the 'City of Lines' series appears on the poster, designed by Woods, announcing his exhibition 'Spaced' at the Gallery of Architecture in New York City.

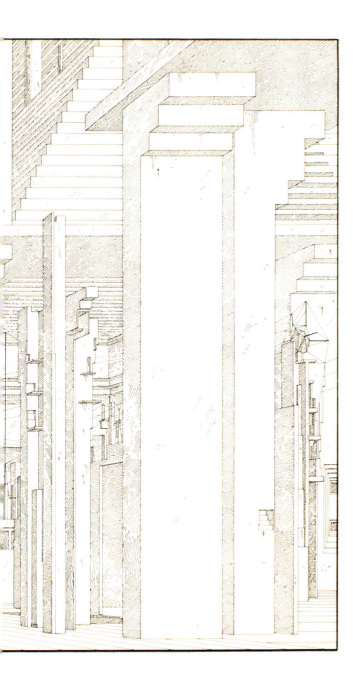

The playfulness of columns and building fragments dancing through Woods's spaces finds its echo in the collages and stilled explosions of the later work

Towards Experimental Architecture

None of this is to say that Lebbeus Woods was copying or even consciously allowing himself to continue the trajectory of any of the contemporary or historical architects mentioned above. Rather, Postmodernism had, certainly in the milieu in which he was working at the time, become all-encompassing; Woods mined it selectively. It was out of the fracture and involution of grids, the oneiric qualities emerging both from the shadows of Modernism and his memories of classical forms, and the mythic qualities of an architecture beyond utopian or dystopian certainty, that he seems to have drawn the world. The playfulness of columns and building fragments dancing through Woods's spaces finds its echo in the collages and stilled explosions of the later work.

While his peers continued to set up puzzles for themselves, searching for clients, Lebbeus Woods decided to pursue a different path by remaining in the realm of fantasy. It allowed him to escape what became the burial of other architects' intentions in sometimes banal buildings. One has only to think of the convention centres and stadiums Peter Eisenman designed or, even worse, the shopping malls and housing projects Daniel Libeskind fobbed off as expressions of deep theory. That Woods was able to make his experimental vision seem so real, complete and influential is a tribute both to his abilities and to an architecture that refuses to be confined to service and problem solving, instead seeking to continually construct the problems we must all live. △

Notes
1. *The V.I.P. Center Shopping Mall*, brochure published by Arthur Rubloff & Co (Chicago), undated.
2. *Ibid*.
3. For the most complete retrospective discussion of Postmodernism, see Reinhold Martin, *Utopia's Ghost: Architecture and Postmodernism, Again*, University of Minnesota Press (Minneapolis, MN), 2010. Through the architect A Richard Williams, Woods was also influenced by the performance theoretician Richard Schechner.
4. Lebbeus Woods, *Architecture-Sculpture-Painting*, Augustän-Xenon Press (New York), 1979, Lebbeus Woods Archive. The name of the fictive press, Augustän-Xenon, refers to Woods's partner at the time, Susan Newhall, and Woods himself (Xenon).

Text © 2024 John Wiley & Sons Ltd. Images © The Estate of Lebbeus Woods

Riet Eeckhout

ATTUNED RIGOUR

Lebbeus Woods,
NIGHT,
'Edenic Visiones' series,
1978

A depiction of a vigorous, impenetrable, wild environment with the greasy tread of oil crayon, sliding tonal shifts and colour rhythm.

Lebbeus Woods,
<AU> (aurora),
'Edenic Visiones' series,
1978

Honing in on the ways in which one matter interacts with another, beyond narrative and depiction.

BETWEEN PICTORIAL AND MATERIAL CONDITIONS

Lebbeus Woods's extraordinary proficiency and mastery in different media was matched by his steady and fast pace of exploration. **Riet Eeckhout**, a drawings researcher and drawer herself, who teaches at KU Leuven, ponders this dexterity. Her focus is on the rigour of Woods's early works produced in Mylar and pastels, and on the carefully delimited spatial vocabulary – agency obtained through the capacity of the drawing to function outside explicit representation.

What becomes evident as one looks at the early drawings by Lebbeus Woods, is the precision and rigour: dedication and determination born out of the critical surrender to a quest, a disciplined wandering through the liminal conditions of drawn space. He can no longer speak, but his work retains its presence and voice. The artefact is the principal source of knowledge now, a vista for our own thinking and preoccupations. Considered here is the work made between the late 1960s and 1978, grouped in three sets. These drawings are distinguished by a carefully delimited spatial vocabulary, and by techniques that lie beyond what an architect traditionally uses to develop and present ideas.

The first set is made with black marker on Mylar polyester film, sometimes along with graphite pencil or oil crayon. The second set is made with colour-rich oil pastels on paper. The third set consists of collages of electrostatic prints of ink drawings on Mylar transparencies. The drawings thrive on the limitation based on self-defined rules and employ a minimum of means to express aspects of space while exploring how different linework and different drawing surfaces can convey it. Testing of the spatial capacity of the line and surface is developed and executed in relation to both process and material.

Counter-Figures
The 'Mylar Works' series (late 1960s and early 1970s) consists of solid surfaces drawn with black marker, juxtaposed with areas left blank to engage in a tension-filled spatial relationship. This relationship – of solids and voids – has an agency. Moreover, it is also the basis of how we experience the physical (built) environment, made visible by the surrounding void. The figuration is established as a field condition, continuing off-page, removed from depth and perspective. The presence of a landscape, of a face, of vegetation, can be sensed. The morphology has a complex presence, its formal consistencies just short of recognition. An elusivity of the nameable offers freedom for other perceptions.

Lebbeus Woods,
Untitled,
'Mylar Works' series,
late 1960s to early 1970s

opposite: The binary solid/void configuration operates in the surface of the picture plane and limits perspectival reading, bringing to the fore the drawing as a spatial experience, rather than a pictorial narrative.

Lebbeus Woods,
Untitled,
'Mylar Works' series,
late 1960s to early 1970s

below left: Introduction of tonal differences: greyscales intensify the resolution and shallow depth of the surfaces and bring complexity to the reading of foreground and background.

Lebbeus Woods,
Untitled,
'Mylar Works' series,
late 1960s to early 1970s

below right: A productive reduction in the drawing's elementary marks, exploring a specific limitation in technique and drawing materials, pulled back from representational figuration.

The content of the drawing is not withdrawn from the world; rather, it is taken from the world to the drawing surface, where the binary condition – solid and void – is extracted and marked out onto the Mylar: a spatial study of the real

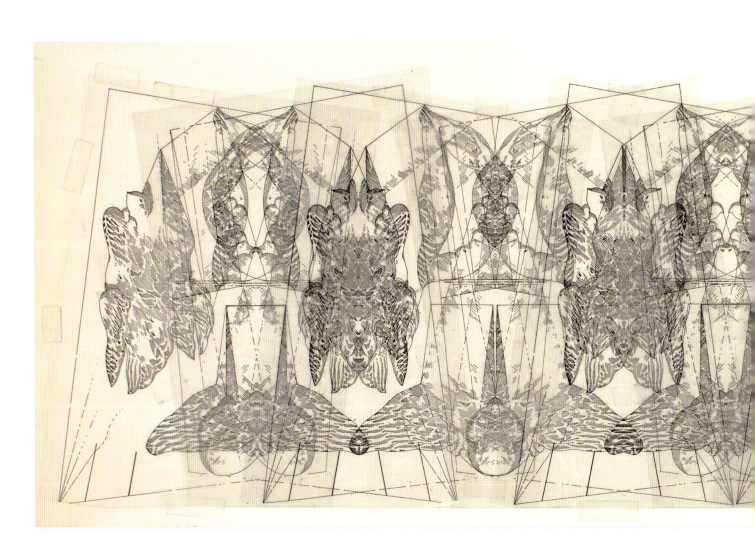

The blackened-out field-configurations in marker would have been based on and traced from images laid under the Mylar. When tracing spatial information from the underlaid images, Mylar – traditionally used for its translucent qualities to copy or transfer drawings – is adopted for its mediating capacities, the exchange of spatial information between the world outside the drawing (underlaid images) and the drawing environment, Mylar itself. 'The way a drawing is constructed is, as in a building, part of its content', writes Woods in his blog.[1] The content of the drawing is not withdrawn from the world; rather, it is taken from the world to the drawing surface, where the binary condition – solid and void – is extracted and marked out onto the Mylar: a spatial study of the real.

The traced figurations are flattened and unified by the solid colour, encapsulating a spatial performance from the source material embodied within the tectonics of surface. For each drawing of the set, a different spatial disposition of an original image is established with a restricted vocabulary. The solid/void drawings on Mylar evolve with increased tonal variations, bringing new resolution and coherence to the pictorial space. Then light and shadow are introduced, calling for a subtler reading of spatial depth, still without representational meaning outside of the drawing. Foregrounded figures emerge from the background.

Spatial-Relational Impetus

The oil pastels on matboard (1/16-inch Strathmore) indicate an even more intense development of surface. Entitled 'Edenic Visiones' (1978), this set of drawings contains an intricate colour development enabling a twofold spatial reading. On the one hand, colour difference is read as material difference, giving an increased resolution and detail to the depicted scene. On the other hand, the introduction of colour adds light and spatial depth to the morphology. Both colour-matter and colour-light work together in refined tonality and contrast. They give a drawing its complex materiality not only as an artefact, but as a site where the viewer's imagination encounters what was depicted.

These mythical configurations establish their own vibrant environment in an intricate but shallow three-dimensional space. Again, the shallow figure-field continues off the page; what one sees is a sample of spatial incidences, sometimes plant-like, sometimes evoking animals, the surface oscillating between a natural and man-made geometry.

While the title suggests visions of paradise, these drawings embody fragments of potent becomings, sharp and fierce, verging on the edge of violent spatial-relational encounters: a passionate momentum arrested in the drawing. The search of how surface and matter interrelate with one another is a search for a spatial-relational expression, not representing but rather embodying the idea of 'Edenic Visiones'.

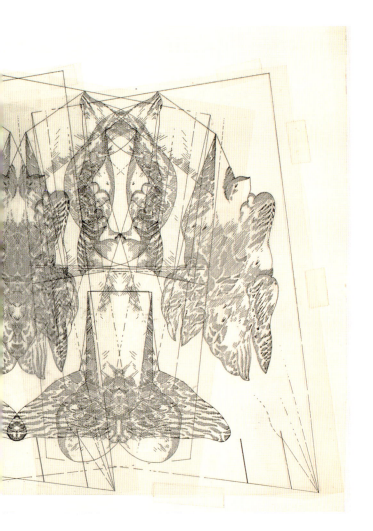

Lebbeus Woods,
Untitled,
'Mylar Collages' series,
mid-1970s

A monumental rhythm allows intense cross-hatched figures to emerge, just short of representational recognition.

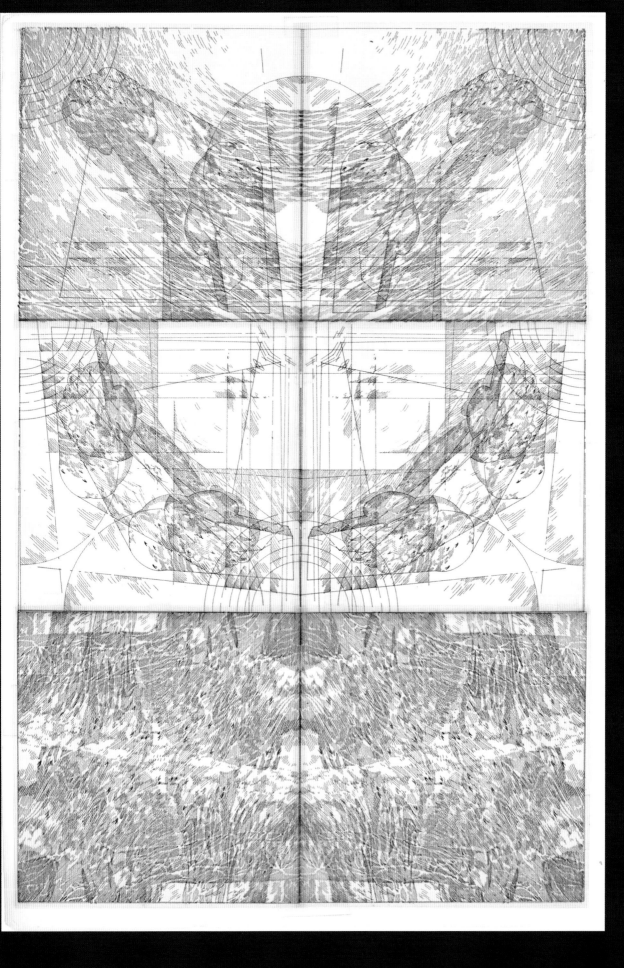

Spatial qualities are allowed to surface before and beyond the placement of things, unspoken and unnameable – as if without origin

Lebbeus Woods,
Untitled,
'Mylar Collages' series,
mid-1970s

The superimposed drawing sheets, symmetrically mirrored and rotated transparencies, develop increasingly intense surfaces in the shallow depth of the drawing: an unfolding of a cosmos, implicit and sacred.

Woods writes: 'Invention and transformation are the aspects of architectural form that I explore in my drawings. These aspects best represent the spirit of our restless culture and suggest that only a dynamic architecture can express its underlying methods and goals. It is significant that nature itself evolves by similar means, indicating that architecture is meant to reflect the complex cyclic patterns and rhythms of nature. The interplay of architecture, culture, and nature, is dramatically affected by light, the subject of our most profound perceptions. The fantastic regions I describe in my drawings explore the presence of light, revealing its role in the creation of dynamic forms and their mutation through continuous experimentation. Color is a primary property of light and thus indispensable in my research.'[2]

The Mylar Collages
In February of 2023, we were a group of architects leaning over the low table at the Lebbeus Woods Archive in New York City. Surprised by the 'Mylar Collages', works we had no prior knowledge of, we lifted them out of the box, carefully unwrapped the protective paper, and looked at each drawn embroidery imbued with focus and persistence. The quantity and dexterity of the work in this series, realised in the mid-1970s, evinces a systematic production and meditative handling of the pen, in slow consideration, repetition and iteration. A surface is built up with parallel hatchings, at an equal distance and with an equal line weight. Gradual and abrupt deviations set in motion directional change in the linework, exposing a change in morphology. The technique of closely spaced hand-drawn parallel lines reminds one of etching. The scratching of the surface activates a planar position in the drawing space, its careful surface movement enabling a reading of the third dimension.

Woods first completed the drawings, then xeroxed them onto transparent Mylar and overlaid them in symmetrical forms, mirroring and rotating them around axes. Collaged together with clear tape, the superimposed plates form increasingly intense compositions. Part cloud, part eagle wing, part sectioned fat-streaked meat – a mythical textural surface, a cosmology. Monumental symmetry graphically unfolds in the taped transparencies. The separate drawings with their ambiguous figuration are overlaid, producing a cross-hatching effect of tonal difference. The increased complexity of line, an effect that strengthens the reading of depth, gives rise to a foregrounding movement of even more ambiguous figures within the emerging composition. Spatial qualities are allowed to surface before and beyond the placement of things, unspoken and unnameable – as if without origin.

In his notebook, Woods commented on the process and on his delight over the unsuspected results: 'Today I printed a new series of images. I cannot express fully enough my feelings for these works. They are images of terrible intensity and grandeur. They arrive from where? I feel possessed. I am overwhelmed by these small pages. They are achieved quite directly. I have done the drawings on preceding pages for xeroxing on mylar. Two or three or four transparencies are made. These are then overlaid in symmetrical forms. These forms multiply about infinite axes, ever changing and becoming. A child's game! But, much more.

Lebbeus Woods,
Untitled,
'Mylar Collages' series,
mid-1970s

Poetic encounters beyond one's own expectation and hope.

Discovery. At last, an odyssey of my perfect fragments. Forms evoking perfect energies, suggesting essential, primordial force. Life force. Of the earth. A universe'.[3]

It is the material condition of the transparencies – the seamless overlapping of the sheets – that allows for the collapse of space, a near-erasure of the hierarchy and distance between foreground, middle ground and background in a perspectival pictorial whole. This is a syncretic process whereby two or more discrete elements unite to form a new and distinct spatial system. All is flattened and activated in the shallow depth of the drawing surface to the extent that it loses representational qualities in favour of experiential degrees of scalelessness. A removal of deep perspective brings the composition closer to the surface of the drawing, closer to the observer, and makes it instantaneously present.

There is a search here, no doubt, for an unconditional and all-encompassing beauty. Finding magnificence is the ultimate reward for exertion. Drawing is ecstasy, a desire to be overtaken by an overwhelming event; a circumstance brought on by trial and fortune; a poetic instant when something new emerges; a dramatic turmoil in which one is, unexpectedly, thrown out of the oblivion of the everyday. It is a divine mirroring and unfolding; symmetry, by its rhythm, brings about particular exaltation, simultaneously grand and detailed.

But this celestial atmosphere is not immaterial and fleeting. The drawing has gravity. The sheets, each meticulously drawn, superimposed with precision in two or three layers, form a weighted artefact, geometrically sectioned into rectangles or squares. This strong structural tie between the drawing and the surface – the tie between the pictorial aspect of what is drawn and the material conditions brought forth by the way it is drawn – presents itself as monumental and inherently spatial.

The Function of Restraint
Deliberately limiting his spatial vocabulary and techniques, Woods strategically pursued an in-depth exploration of spatial possibilities and the capacity of the drawing to function outside explicit representation. This restrained arsenal of self-imposed rules and tools embeds and sharpens the development of content and form. The hand–eye impulses are controlled and ushered into a creative working process.

The mirrored unfolding of drawings, the cross-hatched encounters between drawings, the solid/void surfaces extracted from the world only to be, incrementally, given back to it – are not observational techniques. Instead, it is the generative agency of techniques that enables a shift from the initial spatial intent combined with the self-imposed rules of the architect, to the spatial intent of the drawing which possesses its own autonomy. What constitutes the domain of drawing here, is neither the representation of a build(able) space, nor the pictorial resemblance to what we can name and categorise in the world of our experience; it is spatiality as such.

This exchange of intent, calibrated by the architect, generates unexpected spatial incidences, the poetics of encounter satisfying the architect's hunger for invention beyond his own imagination. What is exchanged between the draughtsman and the drawing is unspoken, unconceptualised, but becomes incrementally incarnated as the agency of the drawing itself.

These rich artefacts can be read as cultural products of their time and circumstances. More interestingly, they are material evidence of formative searching and thinking, perhaps as close as one can get to the drawing mind. ∆

Notes
1. Lebbeus Woods, 'The Dreams That Stuff Is Made Of', 4 January 2011: https://lebbeuswoods.wordpress.com/2011/01/04/the-dreams-that-stuff-is-made-of/.
2. Lebbeus Woods quoted in Richard Rochon and Harold Linton, *Color in Architectural Illustration*, Van Nostrand Reinhold (New York), 1989, p 186.
3. Lebbeus Woods, Black Notebook #10, 7 August – 13 October 1973 (entry of 11 October), unpaginated, Lebbeus Woods Archive.

Drawing is ecstasy, a desire to be overtaken by an overwhelming event; a circumstance brought on by trial and fortune; a poetic instant when something new emerges; a dramatic turmoil in which one is, unexpectedly, thrown out of the oblivion of the everyday

Text © 2024 John Wiley & Sons Ltd.
Images © The Estate of Lebbeus Woods

**Aleksandra Wagner
and Neil Spiller**

MAGICAL
TRANSUBSTANTIATIONS

Lebbeus Woods, *Cityscapes* (detail), Florence, 1978

Complete with cars and grid-resisting statues, this montage plays to Woods's preoccupation with the relationship between art and architecture.

A VOYAGE TO ITALY

Visiting Italy in 1978 as part of his own Grand Tour, Lebbeus Woods was able to see some of the treasures of the Renaissance and the Baroque. The ensuing mix of reality and imagination prompted the Editors of this ⌂, **Aleksandra Wagner and Neil Spiller**, to consider the visual travelogue –Cityscapes – in a similar manner, combining speculation and truth.

Whenever one goes to Italy, it is likely to be cathartic, especially for those of an artistic and architectural disposition. Beauty – both natural and human-made – is abundant.

The Grand Tour
From the late 17th until the early 19th century, a journey through Europe with Italy as the central destination was a coming-of-age ritual for the wealthy. The 'Grand Tour' was a means for completing education by becoming acquainted with matters as diverse as food, art, light – and select geographies of the European continent.

The Grand Tour exerted its considerable influence in the countries from which these young tourists came. Having taken in the treasures by osmosis, some considered themselves to be the sophisticated arbiters of taste, and consequently became its commissioners and shapers. The Italian Renaissance was a particularly inspiring and intriguing mix, made up of painters, sculptors and architects.

It was into this vortex of creative excellence that Lebbeus Woods and his sketchbook stepped in 1978. Woods – then aged 38 – was hardly as young as an average Grand Tourist, but just as eager to experience and record the sublimeness in his own way. One imagines him gliding over the shallow lagoon in Venice, catching the first glimpses of Andrea Palladio's San Giorgio Maggiore church and the Arsenale. One senses his delight in Rome at seeing Bernini sculptures – writhing and rippling flesh depicted in the most non-flesh medium, marble – as well as the joys of Borromini's folding, voluptuous churches and Bramante's perfect Tempietto. Or a visit to Florence, the Medici family's headquarters, Michelangelo's Laurentian Library – its solidified magma-like staircase and its hermaphrodite, reclining nudes.

Woods left no trace of the itinerary, kept no photos, saved no tickets or hotel bills. Not even the sketchbook: the drawings shown here were extracted by his own hand, several trimmed as if to confuse. Were they made *in situ*, as some would assume them to be? Likely not, or not entirely.

Lebbeus Woods,
Cityscapes,
Florence,
1978

Continual juxtaposition of form, material and colour creates a hectic beauty.

The signals of 'post' are the pin marks, recognisable to a witness of the consistent working style: a series may have started one way or another, but the drawings in progress would be pinned on the wall, looked at, taken down, looked at – and only then completed.

Along with the rest, one is left to imagine that Woods thought it best to keep Italy as a memory: 'If I speak, the world will know my secrets; worse yet: I will know them.'[1]

The six visual mementos depict what Woods may have been feeling at the time. Recorded by colour pencil, ink and graphite, these cityscapes rejoice in the cheek-by-jowl aesthetic, in the rhythms and patterns of façade decoration and their various modes of tile and stone tessellation. The sense of vertigo is portrayed by distortions that give each drawing an air of unreality through an antiquated, non-orthogonal geometry. The old buildings appear even older than they are.

The Legacy

The impact of the legacy of lands now called Italy permeated Woods's early output much before the actual travel took place. Cities as palimpsests, unlikely juxtapositions, building-over-building, scavenged materials and appropriated foundations – he first gleaned from the books, along with the heroes and demons, real and imagined.

Still, one had to go to the cradle, and the going had some other important effects. Often evoked in commentaries on Woods's work are the plays of lines which invisibly radiate from the city fabric, but that he insistently chose to make visible. This radiation of lines is a quintessential part of an Italian invention: perspective. Woods drew the Duomo (cathedral) of Florence (1436), with its masterfully constructed *cupola*. This great dome's principal architect, Filippo Brunelleschi, was also responsible

Lebbeus Woods, *Cityscapes*, Florence, 1978

A quirky sketching style, further accentuating the dramatic presence of this engineering marvel.

Lebbeus Woods,
Cityscapes,
Florence,
1978

The highly articulated façade of geometric patterning, one imagines, was of particular interest to Woods, whose appreciation and use of seriality may have been inspired by it.

for the development of a technique without which Woods's oeuvre would be very different, as he relied on perspective – and even more on its distortion – to represent his ideas. The drawings, a contemplative homage, show that inheritance.

Perspective, palimpsests, heroes and demons: is that all Woods took from Italy, from its seduction by beauty, invention and conviviality? The tower, the unfinished column, the melancholy square, the churches and the basilicas – laboratories for observation and speculation – all are there, in Italy and in his work. But, the place of saints and sinners, priests and thieves, frescoes and weathered walls, Italy was, above all, the name for desires expressed through physical and intellectual labour. Neither the past, nor the promise of a future; rather, a parallel universe – an intoxicating present from which most travellers must return to the glory and drabness of their everyday life. All the same: 'One hand makes these marks; one eye fills them with time.'[2]

Se non è vero …
The truth is that Lebbeus Woods did not visit Venice until 1991, and that he felt no embarrassment crying in front of Piero della Francesca's *The Legend of the True Cross* (1447–66) when in the Basilica of San Francesco in Arezzo that same year. And Trieste, Ravenna and Volterra kept quite a hold over his imagination, perhaps because there was something about them in a struggling dialogue with the very notion of 'Italy': the Habsburgs, an industrial port and James Joyce in Trieste; a vision of WB Yeats's poem 'Sailing to Byzantium' (1928) in Ravenna;[3] Etruscans in their tombs scattered in fields around Volterra but made so alive by DH Lawrence in his book *Etruscan Places* (1932).[4] He did not share cheap studios with his expat contemporaries as many 'Grand Tourists' of the 20th century did in their 'early years'; his roads never led to Rome.

To his beloved Florence, that is certain, Lebbeus Woods arrived by a night train, with the church of Santa Maria Novella (consecrated 1420) welcoming the knee to come down. ᴆ

Notes
1. Lebbeus Woods, Black Notebook #15, 19 December 1974 – 6 April 1975 (entry of 3 January 1975), unpaginated, Lebbeus Woods Archive.
2. Lebbeus Woods, Black Notebook #21, 24 May – 13 August 1976 (entry of 19 June), unpaginated, Lebbeus Woods Archive.
3. WB Yeats, 'Sailing to Byzantium', *The Poems of W. B. Yeats: A New Edition*, ed Richard J Finneran, Macmillan (London), 1933.
4. DH Lawrence, *Etruscan Places*, Olive Press and nuova immagine editrice (London and Siena), 1986 (first published by Martin Secker (London), 1932).

Lebbeus Woods,
Cityscapes,
Florence,
1978

opposite: As Woods wrote in an unpublished 1970s manuscript titled 'Views of Dionysian City' (Lebbeus Woods Archive): 'continuity, not order, as human experience in its succession defies perfect form, detests and throws off … containment'.

Lebbeus Woods,
Cityscapes,
New York,
1978

What to do when back from the Grand Tour? The vertigo style of drawings of Florence here depicts the vertiginous streetscapes of New York's urban chasms.

Text © 2024 John Wiley & Sons Ltd.
Images © The Estate of Lebbeus Woods

Lawrence Rinder

MYTH AND MEASURE
DRAWINGS OF THE 1970S

Lebbeus Woods,
Drawing from Black Notebook #22, 25 December
1976

Three figures, huddled together in intimate communion like the
saints in Fra Angelico's *Madonna delle Ombre* (1440–50). The figures'
faces appear as if transmogrified into a bizarre hybrid of Venetian
carnival masks, medieval visors and reptilian scales. The hexagonal
tower in the background suggests how closely Woods's fantastical
mythologies and architectural works were intertwined.

Many of the 1970s' drawings of Lebbeus Woods feature disguised human form. The most classical physiognomies maintain links with a primordial, even reptilian antipode. **Lawrence Rinder**, Director Emeritus of the University of California, Berkeley Art Museum and Pacific Film Archive, explores the manifestations of figure in Woods's private mythology, and points to the uncanny synergy of its themes and compositions with works by Giambattista Tiepolo.

Lebbeus Woods's reputation as an architect is based largely on his extraordinary drawings, which capture so masterfully a conception of built form attuned to the social and physical flux, abstracted renderings of fractures and shards precariously poised as if frozen in a moment of cosmic explosion. While these works may appear to express an impersonal ontological vision, when seen in a continuum with his early figurative drawings from the 1970s, it becomes clear that Woods's architectural practice was in service, at least in part, of a personal, esoteric meaning. Indeed, Woods himself described 'the whole saga of modern art' as a 'public exposition of private myth'.[1]

The works in question, heretofore rarely, if ever, seen publicly, are to be found primarily in a series of notebooks dating from 1972 until 1980 and several portfolios of loose drawings. In these works, buildings, when they appear, are most often ancillary to the figural subject. Writing in 1972 about his designs for buildings that do incorporate figurative murals, Woods noted, 'What I am concerned with here is simply the interrelationships of imaginary and physical realities. Fragments of myth oppose, complement one another across actual space. The gaps between? – merely suggestive. Again – my instinct and facility for fragments.'[2]

```
Lebbeus Woods,
Drawing from Black Notebook #5,
13 May 1973
```

Drawings in which figurative imagery appears as a prominent component of architectural plans are works such as this, which relates to the V.I.P. Center Shopping Mall; drawings inspired by Woods's journey to Florence (*Cityscapes*, 1978); and drawings for a suite of houses and villas self-published in 1978 and 1979.

Bizarre Mythologies

Yet, the vast majority of the works on paper from the 1970s bear no overt relationship to architecture at all. Instead, they present the figure for its own sake, as a symbol, a narrative element, or as psychological-emotional expression. Stylistically, Woods's figurative drawings from the 1970s comprise a diverse range of approaches – from linear simplicity reminiscent of British sculptor and draughtsman John Flaxman's late 18th-century Neoclassical illustrations, to congealed morphologies in the manner of the German 20th-century Surrealist Hans Bellmer, to dramatic chiaroscuros inspired by the work of the 19th-century French illustrator Gustave Doré.

In terms of subject matter, the most explicit thematic focus found in Woods's early drawings concerns the characters and narrative of the German composer Richard Wagner's *Der Ring des Nibelungen* (*The Ring of the Nibelung*, 1848–74), a cycle of four German-language epic music dramas. Indeed, the Master of Bayreuth looms large over not only Woods's figurative iconography of the 1970s but also his very conception of architecture as a spiritual, regenerative *gesamtkunstwerk*. In a 'letter' Woods wrote to Wagner in one of his notebooks in 1975, he requested permission to undertake an adaptation of *The Ring*, a project he says he had been contemplating 'for more than seven years'.[3] The most explicit references to Wagner in Woods's drawings occur between 1978 and 1980, a period during which he made works based on the opera *Das Rheingold* (*The Rhinegold*, 1854). Curiously, it is in these drawings that we find some of his most conventional style and imagery, strongly recalling the melodramatic tropes of the famed – and infamous – Wagner illustrator Franz Stassen. One important exception is *Tarnhelm* (1976), which displays a distinctive melding of High Renaissance manner and technique with bizarre mythologies.

Intellectual Preoccupations

While it is possible to identify the characters and settings of Woods's Wagner drawings, the vast majority of his works from this period remain strangely enigmatic, their content obscure and their style idiosyncratic. Fortuitously, Woods's notebooks also contain extensive textual inscriptions in which he identifies his artistic influences (Egypt, Persia and Greece; the Italian Renaissance; Le Corbusier), expounds on his theory of history and civilisation (adapted largely from the early 18th-century Italian philosopher Giambattista Vico and his intellectual progeny), and indulges in literary excursions into a fictional society that is at once atavistic, supernatural and utopian. Extrapolating from these references and observing in the drawings themselves the recurrence of certain characters, gestures and motifs, one begins to sense a thread connecting the drawings to Woods's primary intellectual preoccupation: the formation of an ideal community in which 'the purity of classical thought and form is infused with the more lusty spirit of barbarians and children'.[4]

Lebbeus Woods, *Tarnhelm*, 1976

Woods employs a red-oxide-coloured pencil, evocative of the red chalk medium popularised during the Italian Renaissance, to portray Loge, the Norse god of fire, and Alberich who, in the third scene of *Das Rheingold* (*The Rhinegold*, 1854) – the opening opera of Wagner's epic four-part cycle *Der Ring des Nibelungen* (*The Ring of the Nibelung*) – turns himself into a serpent by donning the *Tarnhelm* (magic helmet).

The short fictional texts interspersed with the notebook drawings feature characters with a host of vaguely Greek- and Persian-sounding names: Arvis, Anxosin, Antaxis, Aeon, Andivos, Axon. Woods cast himself, too, as a member of this atavistic tribe, taking the name Xenon which figures as a simple 'X' on many of his drawings in the 1970s. While it is not possible to identify any self-portraits among these works, it is evident from his writing that Woods envisioned himself as a 'heroic' figure consonant with the type of noble-seeming characters that many of the images portray. 'The artist', Woods wrote, 'is the hero of the existential age'.[5] At the same time, as several drawings suggest, Woods saw even the most classical physiognomies as ontologically linked to a primordial, even reptilian antipode. In Woods's private mythology, the source of his most arresting work from the 1970s, archetypes shapeshift and transform, much as the buildings and landscapes do in his work of later decades.

Lost Sheep Calling

Woods's world of heroes, magicians, chimeras and ephebes is idiosyncratic and singular, and yet it calls to mind another tantalisingly mysterious body of work: the suite of etchings known as *Scherzi di fantasia* (1738–55) by the Venetian artist Giambattista Tiepolo. Because Woods's notebooks contain no references to Tiepolo or the *Scherzi*, any connection between these bodies of work is circumstantial, albeit uncanny. They call to each other like sheep lost in a fog.

Magic and Metamorphosis

The *Scherzi* consist of 23 plates in a first edition printed privately in very small numbers. It is thought that the artist intended the works solely for his own enjoyment and for a select audience consisting of close friends and patrons. One finds a stark contrast between the pastel *jouissance* of Tiepolo's public painting commissions and the peculiar stasis and dour, even morbid imagery of the *Scherzi*. The precise meaning of these works has never been definitively established, yet one can glean a good deal from a partial inventory of their contents: snakes, owls, nymphs, satyrs, magic wands, burning heads in sacrificial pyres, exotic Magi and handsome ephebes – a veritable Hogwarts *en plein air*.

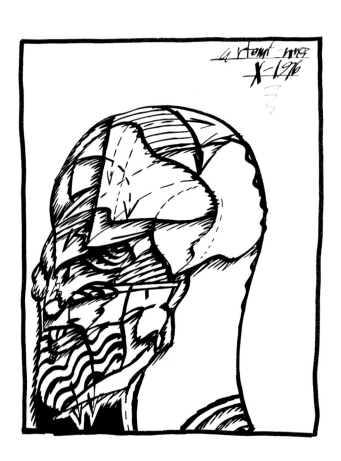

Lebbeus Woods,
Drawing from Black Notebook #20,
21 April 1976

In this imaginative profile, Woods combines the strong-jawed heroic attitude with a suggestion of grotesque metamorphosis. The dashed lines and arrows in the vicinity of the figure's cerebrum are suggestive of physical or cartographical measurement.

Lebbeus Woods,
Drawing from Black Notebook #7,
5 July 1973

above left: Woods's eclectic sources extend to Michelangelo's marble sculptures, *The Young Slave* and *Atlas Slave* (both 1530–34), the poses of which are echoed in two of the figures on the lower right.

Giovanni Battista Tiepolo,
Magician Pointing Out a
Burning Head to Two Youths,
from Scherzi di fantasia,
c 1750

above right: The truncated obelisk standing behind the three main figures (a motif that appears in virtually all of the *Scherzi* plates) echoes the towers that appear in the background of several of Woods's drawings from this period.

While echoes of the *Scherzi* are not to be found in every drawing Woods made in the 1970s, it is significant that the echoes, such as they are, appear in works of various styles and throughout the decade. In one of the notebook drawings, made on 5 July 1973, Woods depicts a grouping of nine male figures in sinuous Flaxman-esque outline. These figures, like Tiepolo's, appear to have gathered for some sort of esoteric ritual or lofty rite and comprise a range of types from elder Magi and bearded man to strapping youth. Of the four figures on the far left, three point off the page to something unknown, very much in the manner of Tiepolo's beguiling subjects who often do little more than point and gaze away. Of particular significance in relation to Tiepolo's *Scherzi* is the figure in the centre, who appears to strip meat from a bone (the bare-bone motif appears in five of the *Scherzi*'s plates). The *Scherzi*'s satyrs, meanwhile, are echoed in the therianthropic appearance of the figures' feet which look rather like rudimentary hooves, an interpretation supported by the suggestion of fur extending from the back of one of the left-hand figure's legs and by the evolution, several years later, of Woods's characters' feet into indubitably ungulate extremities. Another peculiar incursion of the animal into the human is the claw-like appearance of the left hand of the magisterially seated figure.

Lebbeus Woods,
Drawing from Black Notebook #15,
19 December 1974

Perhaps the most compelling connection to Giovanni Battista Tiepolo's *Scherzi* etchings is the peculiarly focused yet somehow wayward attention of the gathered figures.

The *Scherzi*-esque untitled drawing made on 19 December 1974 depicts four hieratic male figures in archaic dress. Stylistically, this drawing retains the light touch though with more sense of depth, volume and detail. The bearded figure on the left, whose sash rhymes visually with the snake writhing at his feet, consults an open book even as his head appears to be engulfed in flames. The overlap of imagery and motifs is striking: snakes appear in half of the *Scherzi's* plates; open books, pages or scrolls appear in six; and we are treated to at least one burning head. A nearly hidden figure on the right of Woods's drawing wears a decorated hat suggestive of Punchinello or an exotic Magus (common characters in the *Scherzi*) while, in front of him, another figure points discreetly towards the snake.

Finally, *Untitled* (1976) is a drawing which, again in a linear style with oblique perspective and including bold patterned elements, centres on four figures. A character seated like one of Tiepolo's Magi on a simple cubic form holds a large bird (or birds). Above him hover two men and a ghostly face which doubles as one of a pair of wings. The distinctive stacking and compression of the three standing men is characteristic of the disposition of the ancillary characters in the *Scherzi*. There is even a hint of a snake in the coils at the lower right of the composition.

All three of these drawings include suggestions of magic or esoteric rites, slippages between human and animal identity, and allusions to transmissions from an adept to a gathering of novices. What are these transmissions? For what reason have these characters assembled? The answer may not even have been clear to Woods himself. 'There are many strong currents in me,' he wrote, 'contradiction, even antagonistic views, inspirations, dreams. One compels a world of myths and heroic deeds, struggles, interaction with forces of the under and over dominions of the mind. Another is nothing more than a series of gestures, some controlled, some violent, existing for themselves alone. Another arises from childhood and seems mingled with other times'.[6] Woods was keen to acknowledge that even when following a thematic or symbolic programme, his own imagery was apt to elude him, slipping into a condition of obscurity. 'I find that the images come of their own will. All the great conceptions end abruptly … I must find the images upon the canvas – no drawing can guide me now, or assure passage. These raw, savage images mock the [illegible text] of my pre-conceptions, but I am helpless before them.'[7]

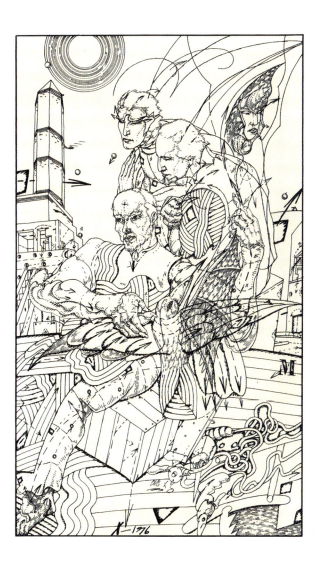

Lebbeus Woods, *Untitled*, 1976

The arrangement of figures suggests the influence of Leonardo da Vinci's *Virgin and Child with St Anne* (1501–19). The main figure's upward-pointing hand recalls a similar gesture portrayed in Da Vinci's drawing *Madonna and Child with St Anne and St John the Baptist* (c 1499).

Woods was keen to acknowledge that even when following a thematic or symbolic programme, his own imagery was apt to elude him, slipping into a condition of obscurity

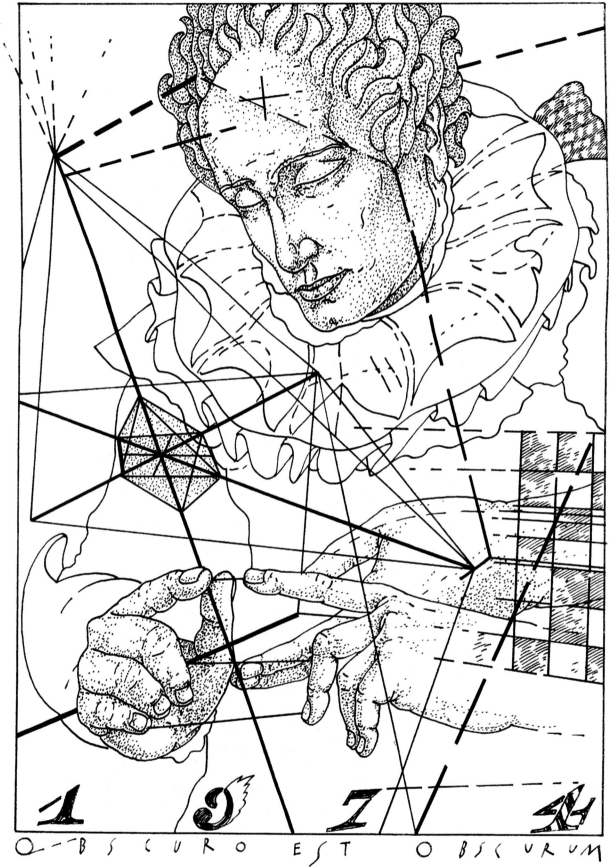

Messenger of Measure

Nevertheless, again with some guidance from Tiepolo's *Scherzi*, we can see a glimmer of light. In both Woods's drawings and Tiepolo's etchings, geometry and measurement are common leitmotifs. Woods's 1974 drawing *Obscuro est Obscurum* represents, I believe, the 16th-century Portuguese cosmographer, cartographer and mathematician Pedro Nunes. The lines and geometrical forms that surround and overlay the portrait are like saintly attributes, including the grid above the figure's left hand which likely represents Nunes's most important contribution to cartography, the theory that the parallels and meridians of a nautical chart should be shown as perpendicular straight lines. This is but one of many examples in which Woods alludes to geometry and the calculation of form and distance.

In the *Scherzi*, meanwhile, we find allusions to geometry and cartography in the repeated appearance of a draughtsman's compass held atop, or in proximity to, a globe. Is the old, caftan-wearing man wielding the compass in the *Scherzi* a modernised representation of Thoth Hermes Trismegistus, the hybrid Egyptian-Greek deity who was reputed to have invented astronomy, surveying and mathematics? Thoth was often represented either with the head of a bird or in the guise of a baboon. In his Greek manifestation, Thoth became fused with Hermes, whose foremost attribute was a staff entwined by a snake. In the *Scherzi*, the old man with a compass and the image of a snake wrapped around a wand are several times juxtaposed. Hermes was known as the 'messenger god', endowed with the capacity for swift transit between the worlds of mortals and gods. In Greek representations, Hermes is shown with a winged helmet and winged feet, signifying speed and perhaps an allusion to his earlier Egyptian identification with a bird. In Woods's drawings of the 1970s, it may be Hermes – and Woods himself – who is present whenever we see wings.

In *Tiepolo Pink* (2009), Roberto Calasso writes insightfully about the elusive etchings: 'It is the ancient alliance between invisible powers and visible talismans, between demons of the air and creatures of the flesh, that reasserts itself in the silence of the figures, often surprised in a moment of amazement or dismay, as if they were faced with the revelation of themselves.'[8] The echo of Tiepolo's never-mentioned *Scherzi* is the space where Woods's deepest purpose may accrue. It is in his drawings in which imagination was allowed to wander – and in which Woods himself may well be the hidden subject – that one finds the strangest, most unique and greatest revelations. ⌂

Notes
1. Lebbeus Woods, Black Notebook #3, 11 November 1972 – 19 January 1973 (entry of 11 November), unpaginated, Lebbeus Woods Archive.
2. Lebbeus Woods, Black Notebook #21, 24 May – 13 August 1976 (entry of 26 May), unpaginated, Lebbeus Woods Archive.
3. Lebbeus Woods, Black Notebook #17, 6 May – 23 October 1975 (entry of 30 June), unpaginated, Lebbeus Woods Archive.
4. Woods, Black Notebook #17, entry of 11 July.
5. Lebbeus Woods, Black Notebook #19, 20 January – 19 March 1976 (entry of 19 February), unpaginated, Lebbeus Woods Archive.
6. Woods, Black Notebook #19, entry of 1 March.
7. Woods, Black Notebook #18, 25 October 1975 – 14 January 1976 (entry of 1 January), unpaginated, Lebbeus Woods Archive.
8. Roberto Calasso, *Tiepolo Pink*, tr Alastair McEwen, Knopf (New York), 2009, p 88.

Lebbeus Woods,
Obscuro est Obscurum,
Black Notebook #14,
17 December 1974

opposite: '*Obscuro est Obscurum*' has no clear translation. *Obscuro* is a Portuguese (and Spanish) word for 'obscure'. *Obscurum* is Latin for 'obscure' or 'dark', hence the translation would be something like the tautology 'obscure is obscure'. The phrase is suggestive of the Latin phrase *obscurum per obscurius*, '[to explain] the obscure by the more obscure'.

Giambattista Tiepolo,
Two Magicians and a Child,
from *Scherzi di fantasia,*
c 1750

In this etching are several of the elements common to Woods's drawings from the mid-1970s, including a prominent snake, a gathering of male youth and elders, an open book suggestive of esoteric knowledge, and iconography introducing the theme of measure.

Text © 2024 John Wiley & Sons Ltd. Images: © pp 74–7, 78(b), 78–9(t), 80–82 © The Estate of Lebbeus Woods; pp 79, 83 Courtesy of Metropolitan Museum of Art

Post-Apocalypse
The 'Ring' Cycle

In the late 1970s, Lebbeus Woods embarked on an ambitious project: to depict Richard Wagner's The Ring Cycle. Jörg H Gleiter, Professor of Architectural Theory at the Technical University Berlin, takes us through the intersected worlds of music, drama and visual expression, suggesting that both Wagner and Woods are critics of Enlightenment. Exploitation of Earth, greed and envy are the beginning of the End, for Wagner. A century later, Woods extends this negative mythology.

Lebbeus Woods,
Untitled,
'Wagner's Ring' cycle,
1978–9

Two of the three Rhinemaidens or Rhine daughters, the guardians of the gold, swimming in the river in the first act of *Das Rheingold*, the first of the four operatic dramas of Wagner's *Ring* cycle.

Lebbeus Woods,
Untitled,
'Wagner's Ring' cycle,
1978

A mythical landscape, probably the Rhine Valley. In the foreground is the famous Lorelei rock that was the inspiration for Wagner's opera cycle *Der Ring des Nibelungen* (1848–74).

Throughout his life, Lebbeus Woods took an active interest in the works of the composer Richard Wagner. The mythical worlds of Wagner's operas had a particular hold over him – an attraction that bore fruit in 1978 and 1979 in the form of a series of 100 drawings and a unique sketchbook. Executed on different types of paper and in a variety of techniques, the drawings are a unique demonstration of Woods's fascination with Wagner's opera cycle *Der Ring des Nibelungen* (1848–74). Even though the drawings were completed in a short period of time, this engagement with the *Ring* nevertheless allows deep insights into the continuities of Woods's world.

Apocalypse

Woods's 'Wagner's Ring' series is the only cycle of his drawings in which human figures are depicted in natural-looking surroundings. However, just like the protagonists in Wagner's work, they are not so much human beings as they are gods or demigods. In many cases, which of Wagner's figures Woods is referring to is left open to interpretation. Only the mermaids, with bodies half-fish and half-woman, can be clearly identified as the Rhinemaidens from *Das Rheingold* (the first of the four epic music dramas that constitute Wagner's *Ring* cycle). For Wagner, they personify pure, untouched nature. But, they can only be seen from behind, whereas the gods and demigods often face the viewer, in some cases even in a close-up. Their faces are marked by harrowing emotions: a restless fear, a helpless despair.

What is so special about the Woodsian 'Ring' is the way in which it portrays psychological states, a quality rarely found in his other drawings of this or later periods. However, Woods's architectural worlds are by no means without expression. Part of the fascination that emanates from the technomorphic and zoomorphic shapes stems from the fact that they trigger sensations that exist deep in the unconscious. The zoomorphic forms are often reminiscent of prehistoric worlds long gone, while the technomorphic forms conjure up a post-apocalyptic future.

Lebbeus Woods,
Untitled,
'Wagner's Ring' cycle,
1978-9

This drawing most likely depicts the figure of Alberich, the lord of the Nibelungs. With his theft of the gold from the Rhinemaidens, the drama begins.

Lebbeus Woods,
Untitled,
'Wagner's Ring' cycle,
1978-9

opposite: *Götterdämmerung*, or *Twilight of the Gods*, is the fourth and final music drama of Wagner's *Der Ring des Nibelungen*. The castle is set on fire, the world of the gods lays in ruins and the gold is returned to the Rhine. The cycle of birth and death can start over.

Part of the fascination that emanates from the technomorphic and zoomorphic shapes stems from the fact that they trigger sensations that exist deep in the unconscious

End

If asked to identify the point of contact between the architectural worlds of Lebbeus Woods and the musical worlds of Richard Wagner, and what it is that links them, there is only one answer: the end of the world. The *Ring* is about the self-destruction of gods and the relentlessly approaching apocalyptic end of their dominion and the world: 'I only want one thing: the end – the end,'[1] exclaims Wotan, the father of the gods, in *Die Walküre* (*The Valkyrie*), the second evening of the cycle. Woods's architectural worlds, on the other hand, depict the time after. They are post-apocalyptic landscapes. There is a strangely peaceful atmosphere about them. It is the peace that descends once all is over, the calm after the storm with an expectation of a new beginning.

What the great narratives of Woods and Wagner have in common is that the end is linked to architecture. Wagner's *Ring* begins with the fact that, as a sign of his power, Wotan has the castle of Valhalla built by the architects Fafner and Fasolt. Here, the role of architecture is only to mark a peak moment, but it is also a turning point; what follows is a dispute over the fee. Wotan is unwilling to pay the architects, at least not in the way stipulated in the original contract. With that, he violates the very principles of his own power. This is when everything is set in motion: after four evenings of the spectacle, the castle goes up in flames and caves in, dragging down with it the gods and the world. Woods's architectures, however, are always architectures after the end. The world is depopulated. What is left is fragments, as much architectural as machine-like. Where architecture and machines converge, Woods shows the end of the world as a return to the beginnings, when architecture and machines were not yet distinct. That, at least, is how Vitruvius describes it in the first treatise on architecture that has survived from the time of antiquity: 'Architecture itself consists of three parts: erecting buildings, constructing sundials, building machines.'[2]

Lebbeus Woods,
Loge and Wotan,
'Wagner's Ring' cycle,
1978–9

Loge is the god of fire and the most loyal of all gods to Wotan. In *Die Walküre* (*The Valkyrie*), the second part of Wagner's *Ring* cycle, he prepares the ring of fire that will protect and at the same time imprison Brunhild, Wotan's favourite daughter.

Negative Mythology

In his 'Ring' cycle, Woods is still on Wagner's pre-apocalyptic side. In *Der Ring des Nibelungen*, Wagner presented the end of the world as a direct consequence of the Age of Reason. The gods, in their arrogant way, are carried away by the ideas of the Enlightenment, which break up their world from inside. Struck by the impact of industrialisation, Wagner shows how the modern world is ensnared in a web of power, money, envy and resentment – all-too-human characteristics. When the Enlightenment turned Reason into its religion, mankind lost its innocence. Wagner's *Ring*, then, is a critique of Enlightenment.

It is interesting to note that in his opera cycle, Wagner anticipates the key issues of current discussions about the Anthropocene age. In the 19th century, mechanisation and technologisation had already led to an unscrupulous exploitation of natural resources. This is symbolised in the *Ring* by the gold lying on the bed of the Rhine. Whoever appropriates it gains absolute dominion over the world, yet such domination brings about the downfall of those who dominate. Modern man is in thrall to his greed for money and power, but the concomitant exploitation of nature is destroying the very basis of his existence. Wagner thus describes a scenario with which we are only too familiar nowadays: wells are running dry, riverbeds are drying out, trees are dying. He shows how progress is transformed into its counterpart, how it turns against itself, and how the great utopia of his present may become a dystopia of our own.

While the Romantic movement and German Idealism clung to the hope of renewing society by means of a new mythology, Wagner countered this with his concept of a negative mythology. In the modern era, mythology no longer has the strength to enable positive identifications with the world in which we live. It is steeped in reflection. The medium for this is the total work of art, which has supplanted religion and divine worship.

Lebbeus Woods,
Alberich – To Nibelheim,
'Wagner's Ring' cycle,
1978–9

Alberich, the Lord of the underground world, longing for power 'up there'.

Lebbeus Woods,
The Rhine, Prelude, Das Rheingold (S-1),
'Wagner's Ring' cycle,
1978–9

above: The primal element, water, from which the Rhine gold comes and to which it is returned after four long evenings of flowing music.

Lebbeus Woods,
Untitled,
'Wagner's Ring' cycle,
1978–9

opposite: A mythical landscape, probably depicting the entrance to the underground world of the Nibelungs.

Space and Time

Woods was fascinated by the mythological content in Wagner's operatic works, especially by his negative mythology. In his own work, this approach is architectural, and as a consequence his 'Ring' cycle drawings are also anything but illustrations of Wagner's operas. On the contrary, they convey a special magical and biblical atmosphere. All is suspended. We find ourselves in peculiarly spaceless and timeless worlds.

The medium for this is not so much architecture as the absence of it. It is noticeable that in Woods's 'Ring' cycle drawings one finds neither architectural forms nor clearly defined locations. What is revealed is their absence. Architecture gives the world a human scale and enables orientation in space and time. Where architecture is missing, space and time cease to exist as independent categories. When they are cancelled out, there is a risk of reversion to mythology: everything is undifferentiated and combined. Woods's rendition of the *Ring* marks the indistinguishable zero point, where the old is no longer there and the new has not yet come into being, hence the confused, crazed psychological states apparent in the faces of his protagonists. In the primeval landscapes, in the deep ravines, in the dizzying crags and untamed river valleys where they are presented, the gods are not at the beginning, but at the end. The beginning of the world begins with the end. It is precisely the short circuit between the old and the new that stands for modernity, 'the ephemeral, the fugitive, the contingent, the half of art whose other half is the eternal and the immutable'.[3] Like no other age, the modern era radicalises the space-time model.

Identified by its Janus-faced nature, the modern blind faith in progress and the future remains coupled with a reversion to mythology. The ephemeral and the eternal amalgamate; the extremes reside in a single unit. Wagner understood this well: 'You see, my son, time becomes space here,' wise old Gurnemanz utters in the great transformation scene of *Parsifal* (1882).[4]

Having broken his occupation with Wagner through drawing, Woods reverted to the other side of the apocalypse made imaginable by the historical turning points of the 20th century. After the harrowing experiences of the First and Second World Wars, the Holocaust, the Bomb, Vietnam and numerous other genocides, the model of negative mythology appeared too deeply rooted in the past. The pre-apocalyptic processes of destruction were not Woods's thing. As an architect, he instead became interested in sounding out the possibilities and potentials of a different world.

Notes
1. Richard Wagner, *Die Walküre*, Act 2, scene 2.
2. 'Partes architecturae ipsius sunt tres: aedificatio, gnomonice, machinatio', from Vitruvius Pollio, *Vitruvii De architectura libri decem*, ed Friedrich Krohn, BG Teubner (Leipzig), 1912, p 12, quotation translated by Anthony Rich.
3. Charles Baudelaire, *The Painter of Modern Life and Other Essays*, tr and ed Jonathan Mayne, Phaidon (London), 1995, p 12.
4. Richard Wagner, *Parsifal*, Act 1.

Text © 2024 John Wiley & Sons Ltd. Images © The Estate of Lebbeus Woods

THE RITUAL STREET: HOW'S THIS FOR "CIVILIZATION OF LIGHT AND DARKNESS":
IT IS SUMMER, THE LATE AFTERNOON OF A CLEAR, WARM DAY.
GUSTS OF WIND BRING TO THE STREETS OF THE CITY AN IMAGE OF THE
SEA, WHICH LIES BEYOND THICK MARSHES TO THE EAST. IN THE CITY'S
EASTERNMOST QUARTER, A BELL IS SOUNDING. THIS IS THE IRON BELL OF
THE OLD CATHEDRAL, PAST WHICH VICTORIOUS ARMIES HAVE MARCHED.
WITHIN THE DEEP, CLEAR TOLLING, ANOTHER SOUND -- MORE FAINT AND MUFFLED,
BUT NEARER -- IS HEARD: (———)(———). THE CELEBRANTS ARE ON
THE STREET. / IT IS POSSIBLE TO DISCERN THE ORDINARY FROM THE
ARCANE, UTTERLY VAIN SPEECH OF THE "ACTORS". A CERTAIN SIGN IS PASSED.
IT MEANS: (———) TO ONLOOKERS, DISTRACTED BY THE SUN. THE
BUILDINGS OF THE STREET, ENRICHED WITH VAGUE PATTERNS (CALLED DRAWINGS)
AND SYMBOLS, SOME OF WHICH REMAIN FROM REMOTE TIMES, OR TIMES SINCE
FORGOTTEN AND OTHERWISE MISUNDERSTOOD, THE BUILDINGS THEMSELVES
ARE TURNED OUTWARD BY THE PRESENCE OF THE SIGN, AND THE STREET
IS JUSTLY ENCLOSED. / IN THE WANING AMBER SUNLIGHT, THE
BRIGHTLY HUED FACADES UNDERGO A TRANSFORMATION, DEEPENING IN HUE,
GROWING MORE SOMBER, AS THOUGH... OLDER BY CENTURIES, THEY ARE
WITNESS TO A MOMENT OF INDEFINITE EXTENTION WHEREIN ALL MOTION
AND ALL MATTER THAT MOTION ENDURES IS EXTENDED FROM IMMOBILE DAWN
TO IMMOBILE DUSK, OR STAYED BETWEEN THE CLAMOR OF THE CLOCKS.
FROM THE CATHEDRAL, A WORD IS GIVEN: "THE SHADOWS OF
NIGHT ARE FAST APPROACHING". AS THOUGH BY SIGNAL,
THE STREET IS EMPTY. ANNURIS, NOBILIS, OBLIGAROS.

Lebbeus Woods,
The Ritual Street,
Black Notebook #21,
25 May 1976

Poetic language articulates the experiential aspects of the space imagined, while the adjacent drawing captures a unique instant within the scene described.

Eliyahu Keller

IN PLACE OF LIGHT

ON EARLY WRITINGS

Where is one's voice to be found? Not all architects search for it in both drawing and writing. **Eliyahu Keller**, an architectural historian working at the Technion – Israel Institute of Technology, examines one of Lebbeus Woods's distinct early tropes: an ever-tense continuum between the image and the text. His ocular reading of Woods's scripts diagnoses their involvement with a darkness of an age, not its light.

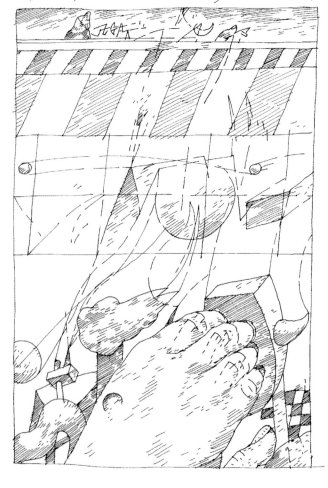

Lebbeus Woods,
Drawing from Black Notebook #13,
13 July 1974

Woods's notebooks are filled with statements directed at the discipline of architecture, often paired with a drawing. Here, the lines connect between the different levels of drawing, suggesting, quite literally, the symbolic connection between human action and its environment.

For in the darkness, lasts that which has been severed
in the presence of the light.
— Joseph Brodsky, 1971[1]

Browsing through the pages of Lebbeus Woods's early notebooks, one encounters a dazzling array of texts: drafts of essays and correspondences, scattered thoughts on architectural topics, or heavily annotated diagrams of philosophical concepts that accompany what may resemble a set of incomplete architectural treatises. On other pages, mythical narratives are combined with lyrical passages, some arranged in graphic formats reminiscent of concrete poetry, while others are interlaced with drawings and lines. Elsewhere, one finds scripts and typefaces that form cryptic texts, their language known only to their author. Indeed, for the young Woods, text was more than a mere device through which to explicate, whether to himself or others, the meaning of his work. Rather, it was a way to think *through* the work's meaning; not an addendum to architecture but one of its essential parts.

Stepping away from traditional practice in the mid-1970s, Woods was formulating his place as an architect both in writing and in drawing. Often, he would take an active commenting stance, whether through exhibition reviews or unpublished essays, expressing dissatisfaction with the discipline he insisted to call his own. 'I must admit to myself,' he wrote in 1976, 'that my contempt for the profession of architecture is at its zenith,' and then continued to critique the culture that afforded such decadence; a contemporary society which 'as a whole seems flashy … a nation of ugly self-satisfied consumers and spectators who have lost all sense of honor, of achieving spiritual excellence through action'.[2] In these formative years what mattered most to Woods was a desire to render life meaningful by elevating it 'to the level of art': not only to dedicate oneself to creation but to fortify a particular position in relation to the prevalent reality, and the effort entailed in 'honing one's body, mind and spirit *against* it'.[3]

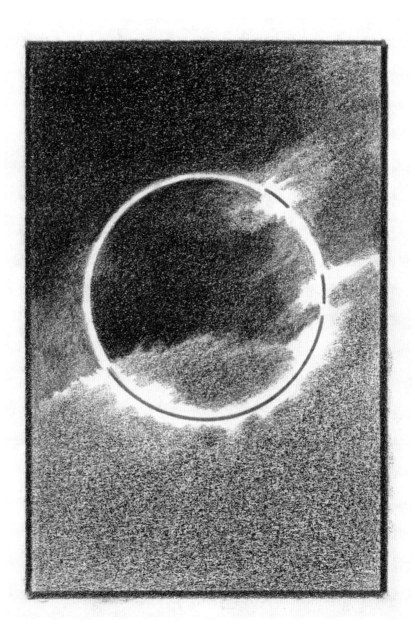

Lebbeus Woods,
Study in Light 2,
'Studies in Light' series,
date unknown

The 'Studies in Light' represent not only the physical aspects of light and darkness, but the poetic relationship between the two.

Drawn Letters

One expression of this position – certainly representative and unique but by no means singular – can be found within a notebook drafted by Woods between April and May 1975. The work in question is preceded by a kind of humble frontispiece: an empty page adorned by an underlined date – 'April 19, 1975' – and three words declaring it to be 'A Perfect Day'.[4] The work itself – a page combining text and drawing – is crowned with a single sentence, arranged, aligned and justified across half the notebook's width to form six lines. The text, gradually becoming narrower, with certain letters marked with dashed verticals or a single diagonal line, is rendered fully in capitals and reads: 'THE CREATION OF SYMBOLS REPRESENTATIVE OF A MEANING TO EXISTENCE IS THE GREAT TASK OF THE ARTS IN ANY CULTURE INCLUDING OUR OWN.'[5] Two dashed diagonals join to form an equilateral triangle, funnelling and drawing the text into a square, where an energetic scribble appears as if it were a page emerging from a printer. Beneath, seven smaller squares are aligned, all joined through similar storming jots of ink that disrespect the limits imposed on them by the orthographic shapes. Below, another triangle appears, within it shaded lips that ask to speak for each and every individual, a mouth that awaits the moment in which the words, hanging only several inches above, will be transformed, through utterance, into symbolic space. The page is sealed with two letters, R A; a cryptic emblem that appears in several of Woods's drawings from those years.

This sentence-turned-drawing should not necessarily be viewed as a paradigmatic representation of Woods's engagement with text and image. Rather it seems to encompass much of the ways in which these two mediums are interlaced and are in fact interdependent in his work. Words, here, are spatial entities, drawn meticulously and carefully spread across the limits of the page's space. Space, in turn, is inferred not only from drawn lines and boundaries but from words and sentences; phrases and passages that suggest a meaning that is as spatial, graphic and experienced as it is textual and read. Text turns into drawing, annotated and corrected, visualising through lines that form a language, the ways in which language turns into lines, only to dissolve, ultimately, back into speech.

Text turns into drawing, annotated and corrected, visualising through lines that form a language

Lebbeus Woods, Drawing from Black Notebook #16, 19 April 1975

The page can be understood as diagram of the process of the creation of symbols. Language takes place in the mind, is then processed through an image-making device, and transformed into speech.

A Postmodern Critic

A quick turn of the notebook's pages reveals not only the original context of the Woods sentence to be a passionate letter sent by him to the editors of the journal *Progressive Architecture*, but that the young architect had in fact practised the formulation and position of this sentence in multiple drafts. The letter itself, published in the June issue of the same year, was a response to the journal's April 1975 issue titled *Historical Allusions*. Described by the editors as an essay penned with an 'authority and eloquence that few could equal',[6] the letter was a call for action. At stake was the use of symbolic representation and historical reference in architectural work, foregrounded by architects like Charles Moore and Robert Stern whom Woods, in his response, took to task.

The sentiments presented in Woods's letter, however surprisingly, were not that different from the ones expressed by the figurehead of postmodern architecture Robert Venturi, who in his *Complexity and Contradiction* (1966) stated his personal penchant for 'a complex and contradictory architecture based on the richness and ambiguity of modern experience, including that experience which is inherent in art'.[7] Respectively, and though critiquing the consequences of Venturi's self-proclaimed 'gentle manifesto', Woods favourably noted the kind of primordial universality at the root of Venturi's proposition in several of his own writings from these years. Not unlike Venturi, who referenced the artistic, scientific and philosophical endeavours of figures as diverse as TS Eliot, Kurt Gödel and Joseph Albers, Woods also noted that architecture has been left behind other arts that have long expressed the conflicting character of contemporary life. Interestingly, however, all of Woods's examples were drawn from textual works: Carl G Jung's and Sigmund Freud's psychoanalysis, Fredrich Nietzsche's philosophy, and the literature of Jorge Luis Borges, Franz Kafka and James Joyce. The architecture created by Postmodernism's forerunners did not carry the 'wealth of symbolic imagery' that existed in those works. Instead, the young Woods argued, they presented 'a survey of stylish, fashionable objects whose juxtapositions fail to evoke a world view worthy of the age'.[8] In their search for reconciliation and pacification, and for a recuperation of meaning, architects, Woods suggested, have done nothing other than resurrect the ghost of a past that is as comic as it is irrelevant to the kind of modern subject forming and unforming before his eyes.

THE CREATION OF SYMBOLS
REPRESENTATIVE OF A
MEANING TO EXISTENCE IS
THE GREAT TASK OF THE
ARTS IN ANY CULTURE
INCLUDING OUR OWN

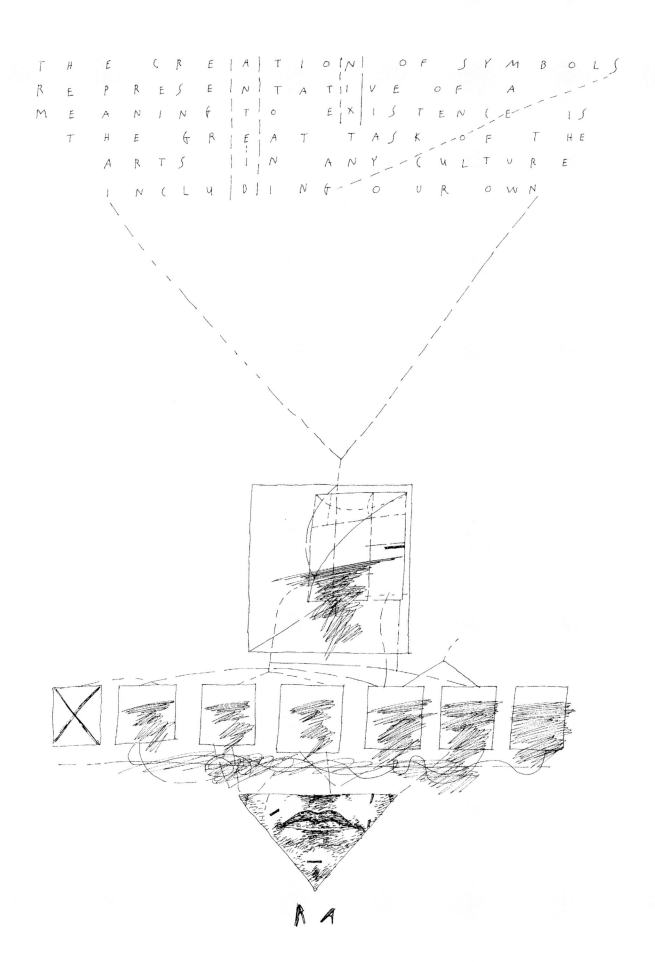

RA

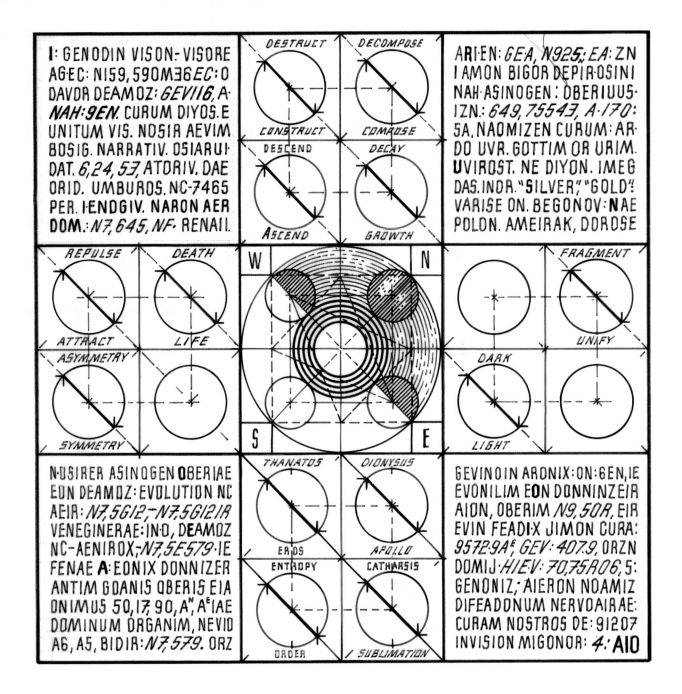

What Woods demanded was a resurrection not of symbols but of the human spirit itself, with its forceful contradictions and battling complexities

Lebbeus Woods,
Diagram from *Four Quadrants*,
1980

The arrangement of nine squares and inner graphics evokes the Greek cross; the cryptic text in the corners Latin script. Geographic coordinates, corresponding and contrasting terms used in the circles, cardinal directions – a kind of talismanic, mythical interface.

> ARCHITECTURE — AND — SPIRIT 3/77
>
> IF ARCHITECTURE MAY BE SAID TO HAVE A 'MISSION' IN THESE TIMES, IT IS, I BELIEVE, TO CREATE IMAGES OF THE HUMAN SPIRIT, THE VERY SOUL OF A TIME AND PLACE, THE SUBSTANCE THAT GIVES TO THE DROSS FRAME OF CIVILIZATION, AND WHICH IS NOWHERE ELSE AS IN THE GREATEST OF PUBLIC ARTS TO BE SO FULLY ENGENDERED OR EXPRESSED. TRUE, THE MODERN AGE — AN ANXIOUSLY PROMETHEAN AGE — PLACES STRICT DEMANDS ON THE BUILDING ART, DEMANDS WHICH TYPICALLY OMIT REFERENCE TO ITS OWN SPIRIT, WHICH HAS BEEN SHROUDED IN APOCOLYPTIC WARS AND DARKENED BY THE BITTERNESSES OF AND A THOUSAND (ABORTIVE) THWARTED DREAMS. THIS OMISSION MUST BE UNDERSTOOD FOR WHAT IT IS: AN AVOIDANCE, A TACIT DISAVOWAL, AN ANGRY AND STUBBORN — PERHAPS PROUD — DENIAL OF SPIRIT. MODERN MAN WANTS NOTHING OF A FORCE SO TREACHEROUS AND MEAN, A FORCE SO BANKRUPTED BY DISILLUSIONMENT AND PAIN. THE SOUL IS TORN OUT AND THROWN DOWN AMID THE RUBBISH OF HISTORY, TO BE COUNTED AMONG ITS COUNTLESS BETRAYALS. AS PROMETHEUS STOLE FIRE FROM THE ANCIENT GODS, SO MODERN MAN HAS STOLEN SPIRIT FROM THE LAST MAN/GOD, THE ONE TOO-SERIOUS GOD OF NIETZSCHE, ONLY TO DENOUNCE IT, TO FLING IT FROM HIM IN SHOCK AND PAIN AND BRUTISH ANGER. IN ITS PLACE ARE STRICT DEMANDS, COMPLEX PROGRAMS AND SYSTEMS DISTRACTINGLY REQUIREMENTS, AS MECHANICALLY PROLIFIC AS HIS WONDEROUSLY PROLIFIC AND COMPLEX MIND CAN DEVISE AND IMPOSE. THE MODERN AGE IS A SOULLESS AGE, BUT NOT A SILENT ONE. ITS LONG NIGHT IS ILLUMINATED BY BRILLIANT FLASHES OF AN ENERGY, ONCE EMBODIED ONLY IN THE ABERRANTLY, AND DESPERATELY, POSSESSED. / IT IS TODAY A DANGEROUS THING TO EQUATE ARCHITECTURE WITH SO ELUSIVE AN IDEA AS SPIRIT. MENTION THIS EQUATION IN CONVERSATION, AND EYES TURN QUICKLY DOWNWARD, OR AWAY. ONE IS IMMEDIATELY SUSPECTED OF BEING 'RELIGIOUS', OR AN OCCULTIST, OR SIMPLY NAÏVE, CERTAINLY NOT MODERN, NOT SOPHISTICATED OR URBANE.
>
> 1

The Darkness of Human Spirit

The contradictions and complexities demanded by Woods in his drawings and writings were of a different order; not a superficial symbolism, but an architecture capable of expressing 'the seeds of self-destruction' intrinsic to any creative act.[9] What Woods believed was missing from the work of his contemporaries was an architectural expression of the 'darker, more savage and primordial aspects of human existence', for him a part and parcel of modern subjectivity.[10]

This want of darkness was most beautifully and mutely articulated in Woods's series of undated drawings titled 'Studies in Light'. Darkness, here, is literally what is drawn on paper, while light, conversely, is simply paper left untouched; inferred by shadows, light is what the absence of lines and textures, of words and graphite, leaves.

In Woods's writings, this absence was tied explicitly to the exile of myth from architectural thinking. In his 1977 manifesto-like essay 'Architecture and Spirit' he notes the essential need for architecture to 'create images of the human spirit', and critiques the contemporary comparison of anything spiritual or mythical with religiosity and anti-modernity.[11] What Woods demanded was a resurrection not of symbols but of the human spirit itself, with its forceful contradictions and battling complexities.

Lebbeus Woods, *Architecture and Spirit*, 1977

Even when they appear in their final graphic format, as is the case with this manifesto-like essay, Woods's textual projects are heavily annotated, suggesting the annotations themselves to be an essential part of the meaning conveyed.

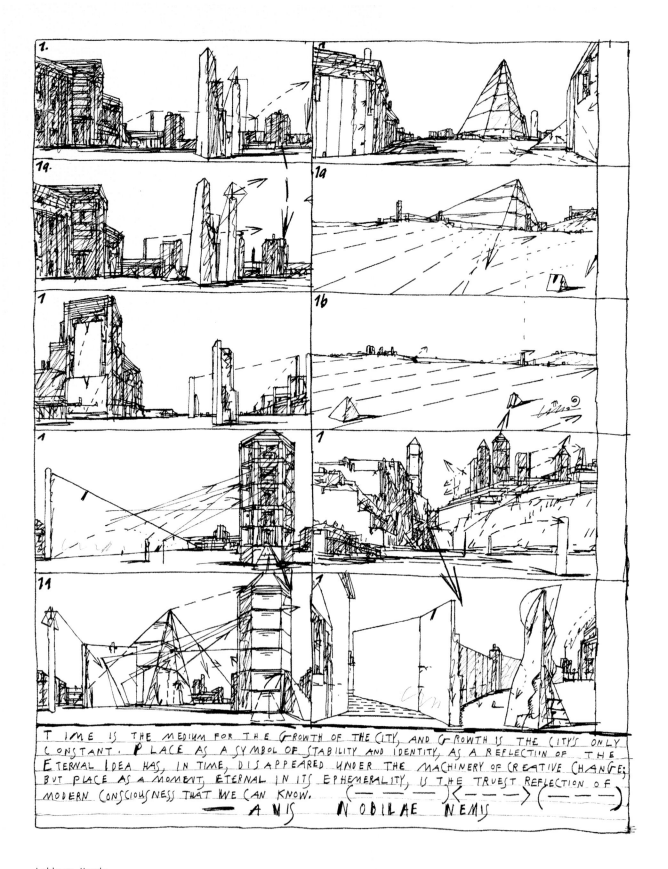

Lebbeus Woods,
Sequential drawing and text,
Black Notebook #20,
29 April 1976

One of the topics Woods explores in his early writings is time, as 'the medium for the growth of the city'. In many cases, the textual exploration is paired with storyboard drawings.

What such 'darker' architecture required were words and language that seek to do what drawings, by themselves, cannot

Lebbeus Woods,
Drawing from *Arkady*,
1968

The image of the ruined and toppled buildings is somewhat reminiscent of Woods's 'War and Architecture' drawings of the mid-1990s. The graphic technique recurs in his last projects, many of which focused on the representation of energetic vectors and forceful lines.

This contradictory nature of human existence often appeared in Woods's writing in the form of myths and poems. In 1968, several years before the mentioned texts were written, he produced *Arkady*, a series of symbolically saturated passages paired with a corresponding set of dynamic drawings. Although arguably anticipating later projects, such as the 1993/94 series 'War and Architecture' or the energetic vector drawings that characterised his last creative years, *Arkady* is a unique work in Woods's oeuvre. Describing the eternal wanderings of a mythical sailor through crumbling empires and a forlorn nature, through 'dark oceans, continents ... and mountain rims, cities that are as bright slabs on the silent face of earth', it offers a dialectical representation that leaps between words and images, between myth and its visual expression, between the light emptiness of the pages and the spatialized darkness that words and lines create and occupy.[12]

A Contemporary Poet
Rather than mere nostalgia, the expression of the inner contradictions of the human spirit and their incorporation into architectural forms, images and symbols is, for Woods, a potentially revolutionary act. In a world he notes to be on the brink of global upheaval – whether due to political revolts or an impending nuclear battle – architects, he tells us, are endowed with a great responsibility as both guardians of human civilisation and its potential destroyers. The images and visions they produce have the capacity, even obligation, to voice 'a call to action, constructive action of a universal kind, or with, at the least, universal implications'.[13] Such an architecture must invoke a world both imminent and never-established; a space, as Woods noted in a 1976 essay titled 'The Simultaneous City', that is entangled within the concurrent processes of change, permanence, growth and decay.[14]

To view Woods's early texts – or Woods himself, for that matter – as belonging to an age different than his own would miss the mark. Rather, from the early moments of his intellectual formation, Woods actively assumes the position of what Italian philosopher Giorgio Agamben would define as that of the contemporary poet: an artist who creates a particular relation with their present not through conformity but through anachronism and disjunction by focusing on the age's darkness rather than its light.[15] Indeed, it was the darkness of Woods's own time that has shaped his architectural subjectivity: a period of growth and material abundance, but also of dearth and ruin; an age ruptured between technological acceleration and exploration into realms unknown, and the slow but consistent creeping shadow of nuclear proliferation and humanity's ideologically fuelled capacity to self-destruct.

It is this darkness, then, that Woods's words and drawings – always inseparable – sought to incorporate in an architectural symbolism that would be both contemporary and eternal. What such 'darker' architecture required were words and language that seek to do what drawings, by themselves, cannot. And yet, Woods's texts, words and passages do not simply project an independent narrative on the space imagined and drawn on the page. Rather, they inject it with the mist that cloaks tales that may have never taken place but have always existed. ⌂

Notes
1. 'Ибо в темноте — там длится то, что сорвалось при свете', from Joseph Brodsky, 'On Love', 1971 (translation by the author): www.culture.ru/poems/30553/lyubov.
2. Lebbeus Woods, Black Notebook #21, 24 May – 13 August 1976 (entry of 29 May), unpaginated, Lebbeus Woods Archive.
3. *Ibid*. Emphasis in original.
4. Lebbeus Woods, Black Notebook #16, 6 April – 3 May 1975 (entry of 19 April), unpaginated, Lebbeus Woods Archive.
5. *Ibid*.
6. James Morris Dixon, 'Letters from Readers', *Progressive Architecture*, June 1975, p 10.
7. Robert Venturi, *Complexity and Contradiction in Architecture*, The Museum of Modern Art (New York), 1966, p 16.
8. James Morris Dixon, *op cit*, p 9.
9. Woods, Black Notebook #16 (entry of 16 April).
10. *Ibid*.
11. Lebbeus Woods, 'Architecture and Spirit', 1977, Lebbeus Woods Archive.
12. Lebbeus Woods, *Arkady*, 1968, Lebbeus Woods Archive.
13. Lebbeus Woods, 'Address to an International Conference on Revolution & Art', 1977, Lebbeus Woods Archive.
It should be noted that the address was never given in public.
14. Lebbeus Woods,
'The Simultaneous City', 1976, Lebbeus Woods Archive.
15. Giorgio Agamben, 'What is the Contemporary?', in *What is an Apparatus? And Other Essays*, Stanford University Press (Stanford, CA), 2009, pp 39–54.

Text © 2024 John Wiley & Sons Ltd. Images © The Estate of Lebbeus Woods

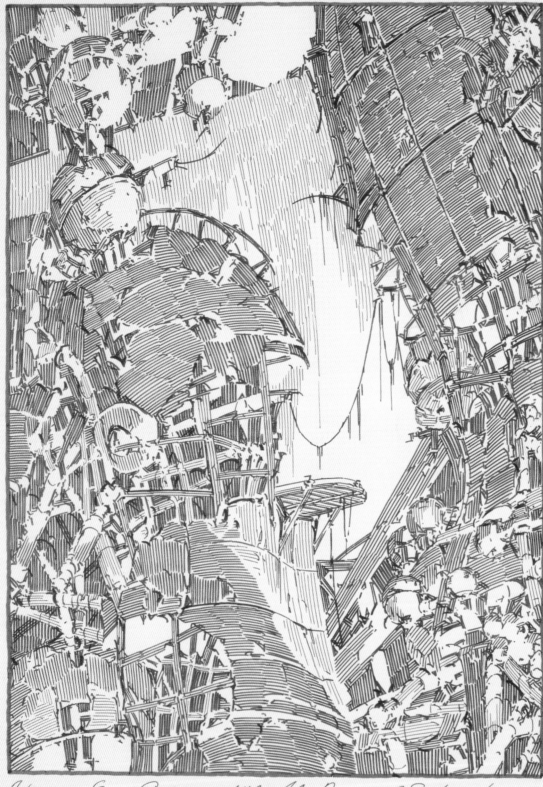

Ashley Simone

POLYMORPHIC MATTERS
ARCHITECTURE, CHANGE AND IMAGINATION

Polymorphism was an important tactic used by Woods to render objects and spaces in the process of transformation and transmutation. **Ashley Simone**, Associate Professor at the Pratt Institute School of Architecture in New York City, explores the terrain where materiality meets change, where fantasy supplants reality. Her prime example is the suite of drawings for the 'AEON' project.

Lebbeus Woods, *The City of Fire*, 'AEON', No 102, 1985

Below the earth, in near-total darkness, is the *City of Fire*. Its bulbous structures of scales big and small are interspersed between abandoned mines and organically formed caverns. The fire burns, generating energy for distribution through a network of ducts.

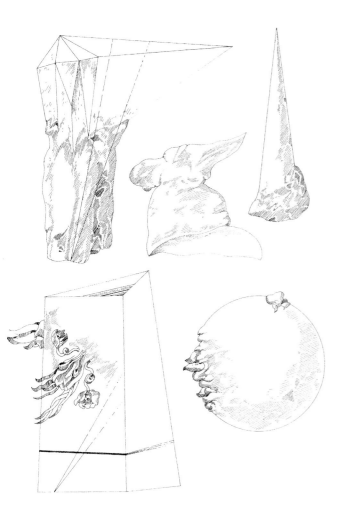

Lebbeus Woods,
Drawing from Black Notebook #10,
8 October 1973

Euclidean geometries metastasise, transmuting to biomorphic matter.

My argument with the vision of Francis Bacon is that it is an unbalanced vision, one in which reason is too important, at the expense of imagination and most significantly of the spontaneity so vital to imagination and intuitive knowledge of the world.
— Lebbeus Woods, 1972[1]

Built on edifices of paper, the drawings of Lebbeus Woods – his polymorphic matters – conjure material and form that is polemical, nirvanic and delightful. They are embodied forms of energy. Static subjects come alive. Graphite and ink become stone and metal. Scales shift, form is reshaped, solid matter sublimates. That which is drawn, and drawn on, matters. How and with what it is drawn does, too. His matter – the many forms of drawings and their subjects – is active, unstable and malleable in expression. It exhibits cycles of change that manifest as acts of and desires for transformation.

Change itself evolves across the Lebbeus Woods Archive. It is seen in discrete drawings made in his notebooks, and extends through a number of projects, including 'Lost and Found' (1973), 'Chimerics' (1974), and the sequential account 'AEON' (largely completed between 1981 and 1982, but with some of the works signed as late as 1985). The discussion of the drawings here is concerned with the multiple forms they take and the matters they address; interpretation is informed by both speculation and Woods's writing. His words lend nuance to drawn intentions, anchoring inquiries about the world, the self, architecture and the human condition. Through an argument at odds with the scientific positivism of philosopher Francis Bacon (1581–1626), Woods intimates that the potential of drawing and architecture to affect material and cultural change lies in moments where fantasy supplants rationality to foster invention.

Matter in Time
The term 'aeon' has multiple meanings. It refers both to a span of time so vast it transcends human perception, and to stages in time characterised by geological, cosmological, spiritual and philosophical development. Woods gave this name to a cycle of meditations grounded in myths and parables he rendered in drawings of multiple scales and media, in writing and through installation. 'AEON' charts progress and decay in natural and built landscapes, delivering us to a realm described as 'transcendent' that spans past, present and future.[2] Time is suffused; as observers, where and when we are at any given moment is indeterminable.

Are the structures of 'AEON' in formation or falling apart? Woods records vestiges of ancient structures commingling with signs of technological advancement, but nothing is complete. Collectively, his drawn observations proffer a call for humanism in a critique of modernity and the mechanisation of life. His words embed the series with a self-reliant ambition: 'we are alienated beings from the beginning, alienated from the pure state of being, but at the same time we can rely only on our own inventiveness to restore us to Eden, to a state of harmony with the universe.'[3]

Woods's critique and aspirations come into focus across four cities – Earth, Fire, Water and Air – that are built 'each in homage to and service of an essential aspect of the macrocosmic cycle of the World and the microcosmic cycle of the Self'.[4] Furthermore, 'The relationship of each [city] to the basic states of matter establishes its place in the orderly evolution of the world.'[5] In the drawings, architecture floats through clouds, emerges from water, from the molten depths of earth, and from rock formations adorned with elements of industry that include conveying devices. Woods's words celebrate this realm as a centre of new possibility where nature, science and the unconscious mind are aligned and man is in control of machines, not in service of them. The inhabitants of this World, Woods tells us, are at ease and 'in harmony with cycles of time and their passage from darkness to light and again to darkness, from Birth through Growth, Decay and Death, and again to Birth'.[6]

Drawings that map the cities of 'AEON' materialise in fields of fragmented ink lines which cohere as form and atmosphere, while time and space are rendered through shifts in density. Woods has declared ink, and by it conveyed fields of energy, fundamental to his way of thinking. For him, the line is a boundary, a limit, a set of parameters for form. The line is a vector, a coded mark that implies force, a dynamic entity with transformational power. Each line in a field holds a similar degree of importance to the central image; there is no hierarchy, but certain structures dominate constructed views.[7] The airspace is soft and diffuse. As one of Woods's notebooks suggests, the peculiar and even light is a captivating and uncanny signal of fantasy: '[A] Time Lapse photograph is taken somewhere in the city. An exposure of 14 hours. When the film is developed and a print made, what is seen is an abandoned city. At dawn, midday, dusk, a city without shadows, without people. A strange light predominates. It is the light of time, even and source-less. … Does it [the photograph] deceive by prolonging a moment unnaturally, or does it provide a look at eternity which is only visible between the moments?'[8]

The ink lines of 'AEON' are fragments inside fragments of time, their duration ungraspable. Is it possible each view, or some, records eternity, the collapse of the past and future onto the present? Through broken lines, light is rendered. The cities appear abandoned and in ruin. But the cities of 'AEON', Woods writes, are occupied, active, operating cyclically and in harmony with each other.[9] One might conclude that within the aeons of time the drawings record, the inhabitants of these cities are rendered invisible by way of the movement required by their daily toil.

Framing Matter
Across 'AEON', Woods's shutter is open; through the light of dusk moments in the space-time continuum of his imagined world come into focus. Dynamism is achieved in the ectangular frame of the compositions, which operate as windows into a vast realm. The apertures onto each city are full, while a viewer is placed in an oblique relationship to the scene. We look down to the City of Earth, up to the City of Air, through foliage and across to the City of Water, and then become trapped – maybe disorientated – in the sweltering, skyless depths of the City of Fire.

The City of Earth depicts a building united with the ground and rising out of rock. It exhibits a collage of architectural styles: from premodern to postmodern. Apertures in the building's geological material are fitted with mullions that suggest this organic matter is hollowed out for occupation and programme; for whom and what remains unknown.

Lebbeus Woods,
The City of Earth,
'AEON', No 10,
1981

A stone edifice rooted to the ground. Is the city coming into being or falling into ruin? A medieval castle, or an intimation of a technological future? Uneven speckles of pigment commingle with Woods's drawn marks. This dialogue likely derives from four decades of uneven off-gassing by the polymers of a viscose adhesive that fixed the drawing surface to its substrate.

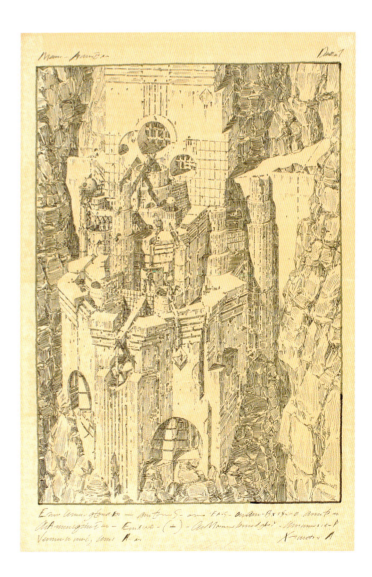

105

Order is conveyed by symmetry in the structure, the background volume of which is articulated with lines formed through relief, and a grid that suggests rectangular modules, implying a standardised fabrication process and the presence of an additive method of construction. One can only speculate about the bulbous forms. Are they metal or stone? Were they hoisted into place to house inhabitants or are they accoutrements of industry or technology?

In *The City of Air*, architectonic vessels too delicate to resist the pernicious effects of earth, fire or water float in skies. The contemporaneous sketch of *Airship* (1981), made with coloured pencil applied to a gradient wash that stands in for sky, could be a prototype for this city's structures. Unlike the representations of 'AEON', the subject here is shown parallel to the picture plane, in a perspectival elevation. Perhaps colour specifies material, with red standing in for sails that will harness the wind's power?

No organic matter occupies *The City of Fire*, an 'Eden' comprising intricate webs of metal ducts that snake through geological strata, conveying energy made visible in torrents of steam. This steam, ascending to the City of Water, parts clouds that hover over a volcano-shaped structure of branches and rock situated on a nearby island. Might the parting of clouds mean Woods shortened the exposure for this scene, exercising selective control over the medium of time? The water marks the end and the beginning: 'the waste of civilization is returned to the primal source of life – the water of the sea. A great cycle of life ends in this way.'[10]

While Woods describes inhabitants of 'AEON' as reconciled with technology and nature, his words are in stark contradiction to the disquieting aesthetic of his drawings. Not unlike the drawn works of architect and illustrator Hugh Ferris, whose shadowy and vertiginous speculative skyscrapers presented a fictive, future New York in 1916, the drawings evoke anxiety in observers. Yet, also embedded in them, one finds hopeful and celebratory salutations to the transformative potential of architecture, imagination and the human spirit.

Woods asserted the potential for an immersive experience of 'AEON' when, in the installations of this work, he interspersed original drawings (most are 20 x 30 inches in size) with their select enlargements (96 x 132 inches), generating an interplay between the original and a copy and luring viewers into a mythical world comprising his sublime visions.[11]

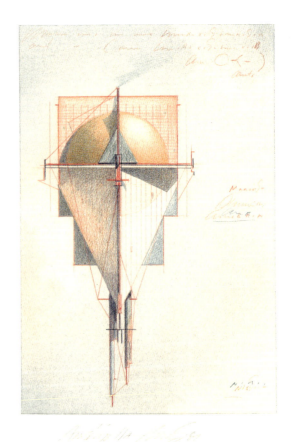

Lebbeus Woods,
The City of Air,
'AEON', No 33,
1981

above: An example of an oil-rig-like platform with accommodation and technology perched on top of it as an airship passes by.

Lebbeus Woods,
Airship 11 A,
1981

right: A contemporary, or an antecedent, of *The City of Air*? An *Airship* rendered in coloured pencil.

106

Lebbeus Woods,
The City of Water,
'AEON', No 101,
1985

Dusk fades in the *City of Water* as clouds of smoke pour into the sky. The drawn rectangular boundary acts as a window into a vast realm. The characteristic indecipherable text hovers under the drawing's frame.

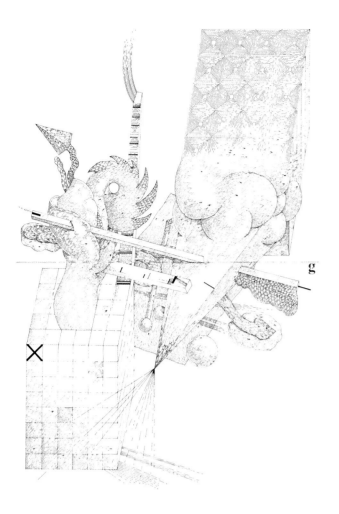

Lebbeus Woods,
Lost and Found,
1973

above: Forced out by heat, biomorphic form seeps out of a crack in a gridded volume and fuses a large rectangular cuboid with spheres and a cone in another.

Lebbeus Woods,
Chimerics,
1974

opposite: Chimeras shake hands somewhere in space and time, amidst metamorphosing detritus of Euclidian forms.

Distortion and Transmutation: the Presence of the Past

Certain compositions, including the one from the 'Lost and Found' cycle, seem linked to early representations of change – of matter distorted and transmuting. These fantasies, however, are distinct from the foreboding and polemical quality of 'AEON' myths. Fragments of thoughts in notes adjacent to the drawings provide context while leaving room for speculation that they are seeds of an attitude: imagination, likened here to fantasy, is a useful tool for apprehending insight about the world and experience.

A page from the 'Chimerics' cycle contains a drawing that affords a glimpse into the mind of its maker. Here, one chimera's hand reaches out towards another; a pact is made. With only the drawing and fragments of Woods's written-up ideas to go on, attempts to decipher the scene raise questions: What pact is being made amid this memento mori of primitive forms? What desires might the powerful yet benevolent figure in the hat (Woods?), descendent of a centaur with the temperament of Chiron, have? What moment in the continuum of time is exposed? Is the present the past? The past the present? Or, do we see in this moment the presence of the past? Whatever the case, the pact is certainly a matter of change.

Germinating in illustrations of transmutation that Woods constructed in the drawings of his early career was an attitude that sought change. This past becomes present in 'AEON', where aspirations extrapolate the delight in his work to nirvanic and polemical dimensions that seek the invention of a better human condition. 𐄙

Notes
1. Lebbeus Woods, 'The Genesis of Form', Black Notebook #GF, entry of 19 February 1972, unpaginated, Lebbeus Woods Archive.
2. Lebbeus Woods, 'Architecture, Consciousness, and the Mythos of Time', *AA Files*, No 7, September 1984, p 5.
3. Carsten Thau, 'Lebbeus Woods, Interview', *Skala*, 14 (4), 1988, p 14.
4. Lebbeus Woods, 'Architecture, Consciousness, and the Mythos of Time', *op cit*, p.5.
5. Lebbeus Woods, 'AEON: The Architecture of Time', *Express Extra*, Andrew P MacNair (New York), 1982, p 1.
6. *Ibid*.
7. Lebbeus Woods, 'Complexity and Contradiction', Lecture, Pratt Institute School of Architecture, Brooklyn, New York, 8 November 2007: https://search.ebscohost.com/login.aspx?direct=true&db=cat06956a&AN=prt.b1244757&authtype=sso&custid=s8440772&site=eds-live&scope=site&authtype=sso&custid=s8440772.
8. Lebbeus Woods, Black Notebook #20, 15 April – 22 May 1976, entry of 21 April, unpaginated, Lebbeus Woods Archive.
9. Lebbeus Woods, 'Architecture: The Mythic Journey', in *The Mythic Journey: Architectural Capriccios by Lebbeus Woods*, exhibition catalogue, Indianapolis Museum of Art, 24 April – 24 June 1984, unpaginated.
10. Lebbeus Woods, 'Architecture, Consciousness, and the Mythos of Time', *op cit*, p 12.
11. Lebbeus Woods, 'AEON: The Architecture of Time', solo exhibition at Express/Network Gallery, New York City, 26 February – 4 April 1982.

Text © 2024 John Wiley & Sons Ltd. Images © The Estate of Lebbeus Woods

EXIT VELOCITY

EINSTEIN TOMB

Joseph Becker

Lebbeus Woods,
Einstein Tomb,
1980

A page from the unique colour study version of
Pamphlet Architecture 6 showing the beam of
light as a red line. The composition foregrounds
a backlit tomb, and an array of celestial bodies
rendered in careful crosshatch.

As the 1970s faded, Lebbeus Woods set about memorialising the great theoretical physicist Albert Einstein and his theory of relativity. A cosmic scale and an anti-gravity mode of this visual and poetic remembrance is embodied in his *Einstein Tomb* project. **Joseph Becker**, Associate Curator of Architecture and Design at the San Francisco Museum of Modern Art, articulates its evolution, marrying Woods's cyclic epistemology with the quadripartite mandala form.

All random journeys
all the immortal corridors
begin and end in the vaulted space
of Earth's night,
under the vagrant light of stars.
— Lebbeus Woods, 1980[1]

In the mid-1970s, disenchanted with rote capitalist motivations and predictably diluted outcomes, Lebbeus Woods moved away from architectural practice concerned with the realisation of buildings, towards an approach more rooted in ideas. The dominance of a client–architect relationship for him increasingly meant that practice alone could not satisfy his desire for architecture and its effects to be anchored in a more comprehensive examination of the world. In the immediate wake of the Civil Rights Movement, the Apollo moon landing and the war in Vietnam, the architecture of buildings (and its service to the status quo) was not enough. This was also the era of the experimental efforts of Cedric Price, Archigram and Superstudio, the hypothetical projects of Richard Buckminster Fuller and the Japanese Metabolist movement, and the anarchitecture of American artist Gordon Matta-Clark – all resisting the hegemony of convention, and presenting an alternative, and at times prudently escapist, vision. Woods knew that he would have to venture on his own path: 'I realized, by the mid-seventies, that I would have to become my own client and commission new, experimental types of buildings that participated in the often difficult, even radical, changes going on in the world.'[2]

Woods aimed to take the very language of architecture and use it to confront the common perceptions of architecture's limited capacities to change. He was pursuing 'an architectural allegory from a cyclical philosophy of history, consciousness and form – an ideal program',[3] creating a speculative version of reality. In reverence to great thinkers across arts and sciences, Woods believed in the motivating force of the heroic idea, and began to explore a kind of architecture that could embody it. He wanted 'to give form to [my] perceptions and conceptions … make visible understandings about the world that have remained invisible'.[4]

Celestial Cenotaph
Established in 1977, by San Francisco publisher William Stout in collaboration with architect Steven Holl, *Pamphlet Architecture* was conceptualised as a series dedicated to unconstrained, experimental and conceptual practice. In 1980, Woods was invited to contribute. *Pamphlet Architecture 6*, titled *Einstein Tomb*, envisioned a monument to the life and theories of the physicist Albert Einstein. It diagrammed a path unencumbered and yet defined by gravity – a homage to the laws of physics and an inquiry into their limits. As an off-world, unearthly and antigravitational manifesto, it offered an alternative to the architectural and societal malaise.

Einstein explicitly stated that his ashes were to be spread in the Atlantic Ocean, and that no memorial should be built as a site of veneration. Honouring this wish, Woods designed a tomb that would exist only in space, inaccessible to the terrestrial domain, calling attention to the forces that shape and direct matter and energy. Einstein's theory of special relativity unified the concepts of space and time into a single, four-dimensional fabric: 'spacetime'. General relativity expanded to include gravity – a product of the warping of the spacetime fabric due to the presence of massive bodies.

Woods imagined a vessel travelling to the edges of the universe yet, owing to the curved structure of space, eventually returning to Earth an infinite number of times. Riding a beam of light, the celestial cenotaph poetically plays with light, energy and theory:

It is a commemorative monument that no one of us will ever see or venerate, because it is gone from Earth, yet it exists in human memory and is the substance of future thoughts. In this way it will seem always to have existed. And perhaps it always has. As we have learned from Einstein, the pulse of light that drives the cenotaph through remote regions of time and space curves to form a vast arc that will eventually close upon itself, creating an epicycle of time and space. The laws of probability dictate that it will one day return to Earth. In a sense it already has returned, perhaps countless times in countless universes that must already have expanded and contracted in aeons of time.[5]

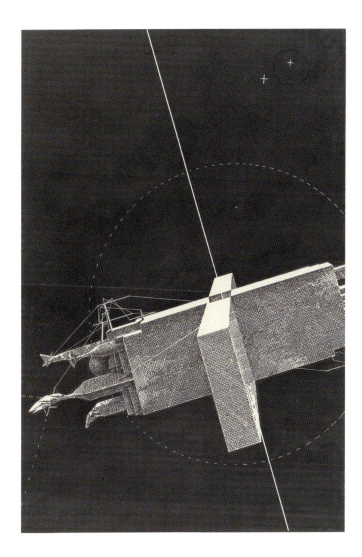

Lebbeus Woods,
Einstein Tomb,
1980

The original drawings are on board, variously scaled to around 22 inches tall and 14 inches wide. The ink is layered but matte, applied in fine tip for the tomb and evenly across the background, its blackness absorbing the light and the occasional underlying trace of graphite pencil. White lines in paint pen complete the final details – the ray of light, the dashed circle, the distant cruciforms.

'Lebbeus Woods: Einstein Tomb' exhibition,
San Francisco Museum of Modern Art (SFMOMA),
California,
2021

opposite: Curated by Joseph Becker, this exhibition presented the *Einstein Tomb* project in its near entirety, drawn from the SFMOMA collection. Carved from solid aluminium by Jay Johnson, the model (1985) gives mass and material to the imagined and drawn, here illuminated by the Mario Botta-designed SFMOMA oculus.

113

Each line and stroke, assembled and layered to create volumes and surfaces, is made with assiduous precision, the marks of the Rapidograph under absolute control

Étienne-Louis Boullée, Cenotaph for Newton, 1794

Plan-section drawing showing the planetarium volume as well as the site diagram. The axial circle inscribed in a square is akin to the cruciform of Woods's *Einstein Tomb*.

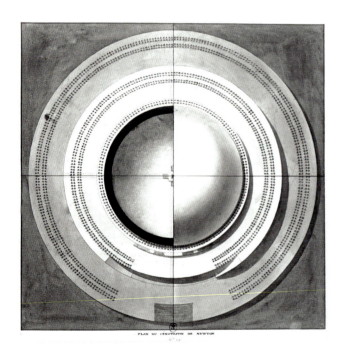

Woods referenced another seminal figure, Étienne-Louis Boullée, a pioneer of experimental and visionary architecture. In his treatise *Architecture: Essai sur l'art* (1968), Boullée wrote that the art of architecture lay more in the conceptualising – the imagining – of its potential than in its construction:

> In order to execute, it is first necessary to conceive ... It is this product of the mind, this process of creation, that constitutes architecture and which can consequently be defined as the art of designing and bringing to perfection any building whatsoever.[6]

In 1784, 60 years after Sir Isaac Newton's death, Boullée conceived of a tomb to honour the mathematician. Reflecting on the magnitude of Newton's epoch-defining contributions – his *Principia Mathematica* (1687)[7] seen as the turning point towards the Age of Enlightenment – Boullée drew a spherical cenotaph, a planetarium, that would, at 500 feet tall, have been the largest structure ever made. It was to display Newton's laws of planetary motion and the solar system's heliocentricity.

Boullée's tribute to Newton was exemplary of a shift in architectural output from representational towards imaginary. Wed to the page, Boullée's impeccable drawings present the hypothetical, even fantastical possibilities of the built environment. These were provocations – truly modern – that paved the way for Woods and his forms of architecture.

As Newton's theory was supplanted by Einstein, Woods's rendered visions succeeded Boullée's; his *Einstein Tomb* is indeed a tribute to the physicist, but it can also be read as a homage to the architectural ancestor presented in Boullée's tomb. In this sense, it situates Woods within the canon of experimental thinkers with prodigious talent for visual articulation. His exquisite capacity as a draughtsman placed him in the lineage of the 'technically baroque'.[8] Each line and stroke, assembled and layered to create volumes and surfaces, is made with assiduous precision, the marks of the Rapidograph under absolute control.

The compositions in *Pamphlet Architecture 6*, rendered to ink-black night sky, are interspersed with drawings showing the skeletal vestiges of the working single-point perspective, a window into the creative process. The intricacy of these drawings, the negotiation of light and shadow in their crosshatched chiaroscuro, the engraving-level detail and compositional ingenuity, articulate the idea, convincing us of its viability. They reaffirm the necessity to first conceive/imagine, and only then to draw. The *Pamphlet* itself, an intimate handheld 8.5-inch high by 7-inch staple-bound 16 pages, is a double concerto of word and image, a complex narrative that brings us into the mythic journey the tomb symbolises.

Lebbeus Woods,
Four Quadrants,
late 1970s/early 1980s

This mandala diagram, with *Einstein Tomb* at the centre, shows references to Woods's projects 'City in Time' (late 1970s), 'Four Ceremonial Constructions' (late 1970s to early 1980s), 'Four Houses' (1975) and 'AEON' (1979–85).

Lebbeus Woods,
Einstein Tomb,
1980

below: Pages from the colour study version of *Pamphlet Architecture 6*, introducing the mandala form. The relationship of word, image and cryptic annotation is paramount.

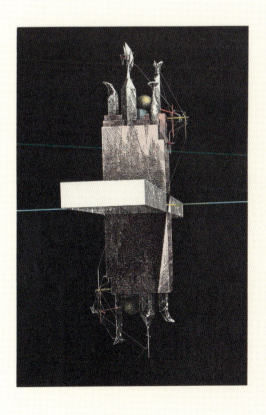

Lebbeus Woods,
Spiral slices of an infinite sphere: revealing light,
'Cycles of Unity',
c 1985

Einstein Tomb is represented in this collaged page from Woods's 'Cycles of Unity' unpublished book project, depicting the tomb's journey through the cosmos. A plan diagram announcing his 'Centricity' series (1987) organises the lower left of the circle.

Mock-up for the cover
of Lebbeus Woods, *OneFiveFour*,
1989

below: A manipulated photograph of the second iteration of the *Einstein Tomb* model, built by Leo Modrčin in 1987. Made of basswood and no longer surviving, the model repeated and extended the cruciform at expanding intervals, alluding to the cadence and repetition of time and the potential for alternative universes.

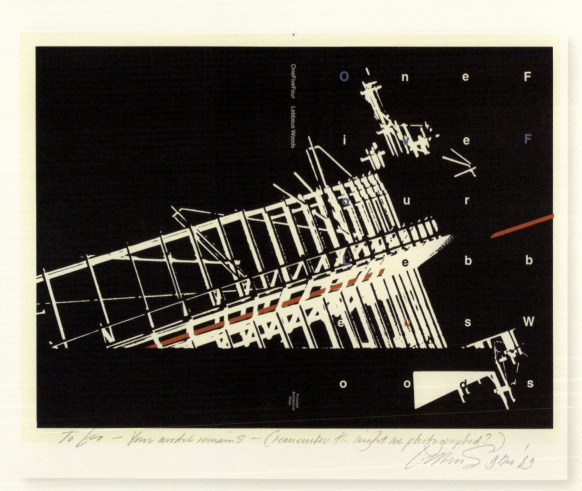

116

Spiral Slices of an Infinite Sphere
The projects that directly preceded and followed *Einstein Tomb* established a devotion to cyclicality, which ultimately informed the shape of the vessel. 'Four Houses' (1975), 'The Great Wheel' (1975), 'Four Quadrants' (late 1970s to early 1980s) and 'AEON' (1979–85) each in varying ways approach the ideas of quadrants and temporality, from the epicycles of time throughout the day (dusk, midnight, dawn, noon) or year (autumn, winter, spring, summer), through the elements (air, water, earth, fire) and the cardinal directions (north, east, south, west). A conversation with – even an outcome of – explorations merging science and philosophy, *Einstein Tomb* is designed as a cruciform: a symbol present throughout the history of civilisation, 'a sign in ancient codices, on countless ritual maps'.[9] The four sections represent the four quadrants, but also contain the dichotomies of rational/irrational, light/dark, heroic/ironic or mimetic/abstract. Set into a circle, they are related to the mandala, often called 'the floorplan of the universe'.[10] Woods writes that the form reflects the 'unity of nature and the oneness of all things'.[11] He compares Einstein's quest to synthesise the totality of space to Carl G Jung's ambition to map the psyche:

> Both men were dialecticians and sought a synthesis of opposites in the creation of an integrated expression of reality. It is reasonable, therefore, that the edifice of Einstein's genius be placed in the landscape of Jung's understanding.[12]

Whereas Boullée's tomb for Newton is static, anchored to the ground, resisting gravity through compressive force, Woods's tomb for Einstein is in a state of indefinite motion, riding at the speed of light – the speed at which time stands still. It is presented as 'both fixed and in flux, existing and ever coming into existence'.[13] In 1987, Woods would revisit the project with a second model, constructed to depict multiplicity and the dilation of time. An image of this model would become the cover of his first monographic publication, *OneFiveFour* (1989).[14]

Throughout Woods's oeuvre is a pursuit of autonomy, a reaction against forces of constraint, an ambition to subvert or reassign their potential. His later work proposes architecture in dialogue with political and seismic shifts, exploring vectors of movement, resistance and transmission. But, beginning with *Einstein Tomb*, and consistently embedded in Woods's work is a drive to both understand and counter the force of gravity – literal gravity, but also its analogues of control and preimposed order. For Lebbeus Woods, gravity is antithetical to freedom; it equals death:

> I choose to declare war on gravity and proclaim it an enemy … I reject gravity's arrogance and claims, and assert a counterclaim – I am a free spirit, autonomous and self-determining, a being and an architect of anti-gravity.[15]

The tomb is indeed a monument, an embodiment of Einstein's ideals, but also of the idealism of its maker. On the beam of light is not just Einstein, but Woods as well – rewriting the bounds of this world. ⌂

Notes
1. Lebbeus Woods, *Pamphlet Architecture 6: Einstein Tomb*, William Stout Publishers (San Francisco, CA), 1980, unpaginated.
2. Tracy Myers, Lebbeus Woods and Karsten Harries, *Lebbeus Woods: Experimental Architecture*, Carnegie Museum of Art (Pittsburgh, PA), 2004, p 7.
3. Lebbeus Woods, *AEON: The Architecture of Time*, University of Illinois Urbana-Champaign (Champaign, IL), 1982, unpaginated.
4. Lebbeus Woods, in a 1973 letter to his partners at IDS (Illinois Design Solutions, Inc). Lebbeus Woods Archive.
5. Lebbeus Woods, notes for the lecture 'The Cross of Einstein in the City of Man', LEP International/Grupo Panorama, São Paolo, Brazil, July 1987. Lebbeus Woods Archive.
6. Étienne-Louis Boullée, Helen Rosenau and Sheila de Vallée, *Architecture: Essay on Art* [1968], Academy Editions (London), 1976, p 83.
7. Isaac Newton, Andrew Motte and NW Chittenden, *Newton's Principia: The Mathematical Principles of Natural Philosophy*, D Adee (New York), 1848.
8. Geoff Manaugh, 'Without Walls: An Interview with Lebbeus Woods', BLDGBLOG, 3 October 2007: www.bldgblog.com/2007/10/without-walls-an-interview-with-lebbeus-woods/.
9. Lebbeus Woods, *Pamphlet Architecture 6, op cit*.
10. Asia Society, 'Mandala: The Architecture of Enlightenment': https://asiasociety.org/mandala-architecture-enlightenment.
11. Lebbeus Woods, *Pamphlet Architecture 6, op cit*.
12. Lebbeus Woods, *AEON, op cit*.
13. *Ibid*.
14. Lebbeus Woods, *OneFiveFour*, Princeton Architectural Press (New York), 1989.
15. Lebbeus Woods, *ANARCHITECTURE: Architecture Is a Political Act*, Architectural Monographs 22, Academy Editions (London), 1992, p 64.

His later work proposes architecture in dialogue with political and seismic shifts, exploring vectors of movement, resistance and transmission

Text © 2024 John Wiley & Sons Ltd. Images: © pp 110–11, 112–13, 115(b) © The Estate of Lebbeus Woods. Courtesy of SFMOMA; p 114 © Photo 12 / Alamy Stock Photo; pp 115(t), 116(t) © The Estate of Lebbeus Woods; p 116(b) Image courtesy Leo Modrčin © The Estate of Lebbeus Woods

Peter Cook

Catalytic Moments, Friendships and Journeys

When an architectural argonaut whose creative life was spent on a quest to open more possibilities for architecture meets another, a special mutual respect is instilled. **Peter Cook**, Archigram co-founder and doyen of the Architectural Association (AA) in the 1980s, recalls his initial encounter and some of the moments he has shared with Lebbeus Woods over the decades.

Lebbeus Woods, *Untitled*, 1970s

This essay is a personal account of the initial encounter and some of the subsequent meetings between Lebbeus Woods and Peter Cook. These metamorphic heads are analogous to their creative dialogue and its dynamic reciprocity.

Sometime in 1984, Zaha Hadid introduced a friend that she had met in New York to an evening audience at the Architectural Association (AA) in London. The link had probably been that of Steven Holl, who had hosted this guy, Lebbeus Woods, on the pages of *Pamphlet Architecture*.[1]

It says something of the insular world of architecture that this architectural publication series, which has over the years been the first to display support for a wide range of positions and ideas, is hardly known outside New York.

By the same connection, Lebbeus Woods had held a show of drawings at Storefront for Art and Architecture in New York.[2] Again – at that time – a rather original but niche institution.

It was surely Zaha's overt support for this mystery person that drew us into the room. As I watched, I was thrilled, excited, inspired (and not a little jealous) of his images of floating 'castles' and vivid constructs – more excited than at any moment since the Archigram days, or perhaps my first sight of Tokyo. Uncharacteristically, I think, I erupted at the end of the lecture with not a question from the floor, but a paean of enthusiasm. Frothing and bubbling, I greeted him as 'one of us', but of course he was much more. Notwithstanding his looks and his persona that stood apart from the typical interesting young architect that you would encounter in London, Berlin or Vienna. No black uniform, or subtle blend of Che Guevara and latter-day Montmartre, but a neat – rather conservative – grey suit plus the cigarette holder and the elegant wife. His language, emitted via the gravelly but eminently polite manner of the Midwest, was earnest but not shrill. In another world, you could have mistaken him for a sympathetic bank manager.

Lebbeus Woods,
'Cycles of Transformation:
Four Cities and Beyond'
lecture notes,
Architectural Association (AA),
London,
7 February 1984

Page 1 of the lecture presented the evening Cook and Woods first met.

Lecture @ AA 1984

My presentation will be something of a travelogue--a journey through time. I have promised you a look at the Future, and I hope what you see will have meaning for the Present, too.

(1) The Present--it is only a thin moving line of time separating the dark gulfs of Past and Future, twin abysses opening on either side of a tenuous moment.

(2) This thin path, this narrow landscape of the Present is lit not so much by conscious thought as by sensation, since we move through it too quickly to grasp its substance.

(3) We must be content to cast our conscious thought ever backward on the moment that has just passed--on the landscape of the Past--or, as we like to say, (4) forward, onto the landscape of the Future.

But both these regions are dim and the searching beam of consciousness is weak and cannot penetrate very deeply in either direction.

(5) Traversing this vast landscape of time is a dangerous, difficult task. On skill and luck and courage our survival depends.

(6) I do not, as you may guess, see much difference between speculation about the Past--called Romance and history--and speculation about the Future--(7) called fantasy or prophesy.

Neither Past nor Future exist concretely in the Present. Both are known to us only by inference. (8) Both contain meanings and signs and portents for the Present, even as it slips quickly into Past, or Future, or both.

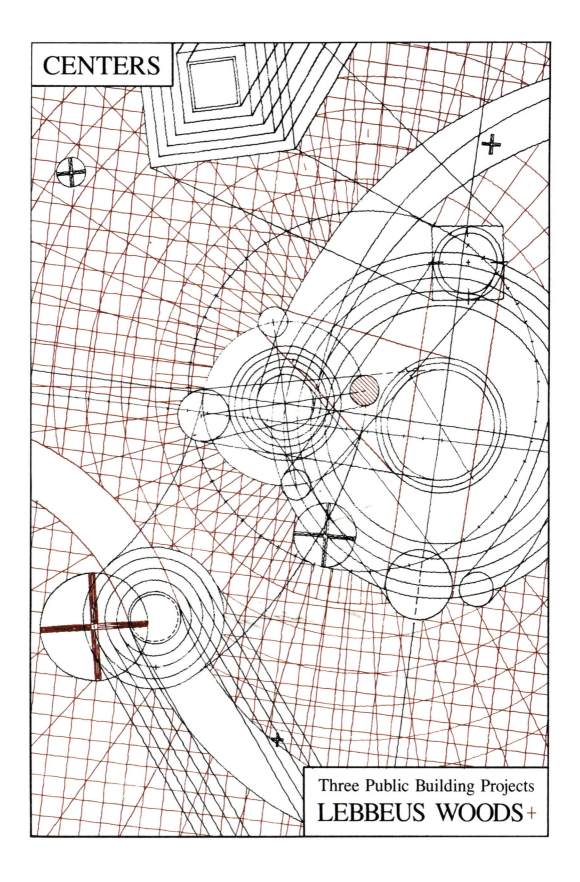

Lebbeus Woods,
Cover of CENTERS: Three Public Building Projects,
1984

This small publication was created to coincide with Woods's exhibition at Storefront for Art and Architecture in New York. Its title affirms his preoccupation with an age he sees as characterised not by a unity, but the many.

Lebbeus Woods,
Tower,
date unknown

Most architects harbour ambitions to design towers; Woods was a master of the genre. This drawing shows either the rocky outcrop on which the tower sits, or perhaps two men in conversation.

Lebbeus Woods,
Tower B,
1981

Set amongst an implied urban context, the tower formally transitions from a relatively traditional base, as it rises, to fragmented mesa-like structures at its zenith.

In the light of the narrowness and sluggishness of both the British and American mainstream we realised that we could only use the rhetoric of invented projects and drawings

But it was the power of those drawings – they took your breath away. Propositions with the drama of Gulliver, Jules Verne, Dan Dare, Superman (name your favourite) drawn with a combination of finesse and near preposterousness but also with a beguiling patination. The armatures really did look to be engineered, the surfaces slightly worn by impact with the elements, the fixings logical, the colour (if used) naturalist rather than emblemic.

A conversation at the bar (the first of many at bars and restaurants around the world) immediately revealed our somewhat similar views on the architectural scene around us. In the light of the narrowness and sluggishness of both the British and American mainstream we realised that we could only use the rhetoric of invented projects and drawings. It was only later that Leb, as friends called him, would reveal his strength of purpose through writings and very strategically posed books containing both an amazing graphicacity and the disturbing but sophisticated use of language.

Lebbeus in New York
His early work in New York City was on the construction of the Ford Foundation building (completed 1967) and there is reason to believe that he was well versed in structural and constructional lore, having studied engineering at Purdue University in Indiana as well as architecture at the University of Illinois Urbana-Champaign. After he permanently settled on the island of Manhattan, in 1976, his drawing skills came to the notice of Eugene Kohn of architectural practice Kohn Pedersen Fox, and the regular commissioning of perspective drawings for this firm (and some others) became daily means of sustenance. By the time I visited him, Lebbeus lived in a small but eminently located apartment on the Upper East Side, facing the back of *Penthouse* magazine owner Bob Guccione's house. There was no formal 'studio' there, but enough flat surfaces for making drawings. Life was not overly extravagant: except in the direction of Champagne and eating out. You could gauge the state of play by the fridge: Krug on the good days and a dodgy label (but never Prosecco) on the bad.

Later – in one of the 'good' periods – Leb would have you collected and driven in a Cadillac over to Pratt Institute, where he was also teaching more regularly in the mid- and later 1980s. Again, in tight moments, the chauffeur, named Eugene, and the caddy were conspicuously absent. Not that he seemed to be suffering since, eventually, the good times would reappear. It was undoubtedly a question of style.

If we extrapolate this, we can see a certain parallel between the life and dreams of Lebbeus Woods, crossing from this lifestyle to the world of the drawings. Both were fully aspirational. Both were exotic to the extent of lived-out urbanity and visualised extremity.

Why stop short on either front? There was a hint of F Scott Fitzgerald about it all.

Other connections led to John Hejduk, Raimund Abraham and Michael Webb at the Cooper Union and to younger teachers there such as Ricardo Scofidio, Elizabeth Diller and Diane Lewis. That this circle of like-minded people would eventually replace the commercial world would become almost inevitable. On the other hand, Lebbeus remarked that Peter Eisenman would stare through him in the Cooper Union elevator, which, more than a statement of fact, was coded information, revealing that the intricate network of Ivy League architect-academics who for two or three decades had been manipulated by Godfather Philip Johnson and immaculately developed by Eisenman would never recognise him.

This studied ignorance of his work lasted until and beyond the event of the heavily publicised Yale Conference of February 2012, entitled 'Is Drawing Dead?'. Michael Graves, Massimo Scolari, Greg Lynn and a heavyweight audience – but no Lebbeus Woods (a mere 62 miles away). Knowing this, I loaded a good chunk of Leborama into my own keynote address; it still elicited no response.

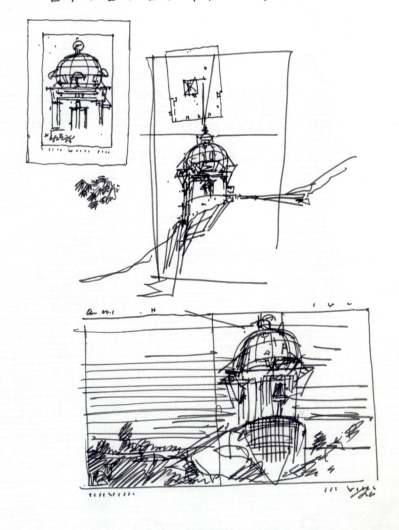

Lebbeus Woods,
Center for New Technology,
Montage 1,
1985

left: Chairman of the Architectural Association (AA) from 1971 to 1990, Alvin Boyarsky was a great supporter of Cook as well as Woods during this halcyon era. This drawing from Boyarsky's extensive architectural collection was exhibited at Woods's first London show – 'Origins' – held at the AA from 27 September to 26 October 1985.

Lebbeus Woods,
Sketches for the Epicyclarium,
1984

opposite: One can see the initial ideas for *Epicyclarium*, a temple-like scheme based on Woods's mandalic forms, the circle and the 'plus' sign – a place of introspection encouraging the mixing of all manner of human knowledge.

Europe and Academe

Meanwhile the computer had very much arrived both in academe and even more vehemently in the commercial office. Lebbeus's hand-drawn renderings were expensive, idiosyncratic and nominally archaic. A parallel reason for his abandonment of this activity was his increasing presence in architectural journals and on university platforms. Rumours of the AA evening made it over to Oslo, over to Amsterdam and then to Berlin, where his work was picked up by the Aedes Galerie; then to Vienna and Frankfurt where, at the Städelschule, he became a regular attraction. At University College London's Bartlett School of Architecture, too, where his frowned-upon demands (for £1,000 in notes in an envelope, a *good* hotel and victualling up to his standards) were fantastic value by the time that a stonking, full-on, inspirational lecture had eclipsed even his last stonker and revealed even more extraordinary drawings.

At the other end of the scale, he would sit down with a dozen or so students and show them how to make a perspective – in simple steps – in half an hour. His lethal combination of clarity and seriousness as a critic could make teachers feel inadequate in the face of such sage-like commonsense that could sometimes even head into the territory of piety.

The European encounters eventually took many forms and the drama of some of his experiences shows clearly in some of his key drawings: objects come under attack, hybrids are almost building-as-rocket. In November of 1993, Lebbeus travelled into the besieged city of Sarajevo, brought with him his second *Pamphlet*,[3] and returned there again in 1994 to teach the city's architecture students with Thom Mayne. His experiences helped define his strong belief in humanity and the strength of commitment and conviction, his 'take' on experimental architecture becoming both moral- and narrative-based.

RIEA

The First Conference

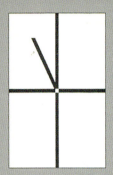

Peter Cook
Lise Anne Couture
Neil Denari
Gordon Gilbert
Ken Kaplan
Ted Krueger
Hani Rashid
Michael Sorkin
Michael Webb
Lebbeus Woods

Aedes
Princeton Architectural Press

The new breed of drawing people are surely the progeny of Lebbeus's work. Even if they have different techniques or fetishes, it is the thrust forward and combinations of experiment and vision that suggest their alliance

Later yet, in the very early 2000s, very much buoyed up by the support of the new Dean of Architecture at Cooper, Anthony Vidler, Lebbeus entered a very creative period on all fronts.

In his last years, Leb circulated a famous blog – read by many young architects. Even from a wheelchair his voice was strong. His books became simultaneously collectors' items and artworks in themselves. Through them we encountered his metamorphosis from the layered and surfaced and loaded, to the sparse and the stringy and the spatial. Thus, in the 2002/03 Paris show 'Unknown Quantity', curated by Paul Virilio,[4] we were able to walk through the Woodsian cascades of thin aluminium rods that built up to virtual clouds of territory. Drawings contemporary with the show exposed this new preoccupation.

Beyond NYC: SCI-Arc and the Research Institute for Experimental Architecture
Two incidents may serve to illustrate both the independence and the fragility of Leb's position. I clearly recall a jolly moment of 1997, under a thatch awning in the Hawaiian style somewhere among the moorings of Marina del Ray in Los Angeles. I was having lunch with him and the architect Neil Denari, having been forced to write pretty much equal letters of support for both for the job of Director of the Southern California Institute of Architecture (SCI-Arc) – a place for which I have enduring affection. What else could I do? They were great creatives, serious thinkers and inventors: I knew that *one* of them would get it. The atmosphere was good, not loaded. They were able to recognise each other's serious intent and, in a way, common interest. It was Neil who won the position. Characteristically, his first act was to offer Lebbeus the job of running the school's European outfit in Vico Morcote, Switzerland, giving him a breathing space.

Of course, Neil was included in the 1989 roundup of characters along with Lise Anne Couture, Gordon Gilbert, Ken Kaplan, Ted Krueger, Hani Rashid, Michael Sorkin, Michael Webb and myself to take part in a beautiful séance-like event, held at Emmons Farms, Oneonta, Upstate New York. It was a meeting of the Research Institute for Experimental Architecture (RIEA), co-founded in 1988 by Lebbeus and Olive Brown. In a large, dark barn we all quietly exposed our latest architectural positions. It was a meeting, if you like, of co-conspirators. Its outcome was captured in an exhibition – 'RIEA: The First Conference' – at the Aedes Galerie in February and March 1990, and through the accompanying publication.[5]

Cover of *RIEA: The First Conference* exhibition catalogue, Berlin, 1990

The catalogue and the exhibition, sponsored by the Aedes Architecture Forum and Princeton Architectural Press, were the sum of the First Conference convened by the Research Institute for Experimental Architecture (RIEA). Away from the academic institutions, offices and students that often choreographed their lives, the gathering was designed as a reflective discussion among peers on where experimental architectural design might go in the near future.

Recognition Through Peers and Books
I cannot resist adding a telling incident regarding Lebbeus's influence. Somewhere around 2010 I was killing time in a small but upmarket fashion centre in Tel Aviv (my wife's city). A minor branch of Steimatzky's suddenly disclosed a row of Lebbeus Woods's books. Hardly any other architecture books and a clientele of the buyers of smart pants or Boss trousers. What was going on? Yet somewhere, somewhere, in the bowels of the Steimatzky's warehouse was a Woods fan. A Star Wars fanatic? A nutter? A bored architecture student? Somebody trying to say something – unwittingly signalling to this frothing and bubbling admirer in a place no less appropriate than the AA, perhaps?

The new breed of drawing people are surely the progeny of Lebbeus's work. Even if they have different techniques or fetishes, it is the thrust forward and combinations of experiment and vision that suggest their alliance. Only Walter Pichler and the Austrians now demand a similar moment of celebration.

Oh, for the grunts and growls of Lebbeus Woods and Raimund Abraham, late over wine somewhere off Bleecker Street.

Notes
1. Lebbeus Woods, *Pamphlet Architecture 6: Einstein Tomb*, William Stout Publishers (San Francisco, CA), 1980.
2. Lebbeus Woods, *CENTERS: Three Public Building Projects*, exhibition at Storefront for Art and Architecture, New York, 8 November–2 December 1984.
3. Lebbeus Woods, *Pamphlet Architecture 15: War and Architecture*, Princeton Architectural Press (New York), 1993.
4. Paul Virilio, *Unknown Quantity*, exhibition catalogue, Fondation Cartier pour l'art contemporain and Thames & Hudson (New York), 2002.
5. Peter Cook *et al*, *RIEA: The First Conference*, Aedes Architecture Forum and Princeton Architectural Press (New York), 1990.

Text © 2024 John Wiley & Sons Ltd. Images: pp 118–23, 124(l), 126 © The Estate of Lebbeus Woods; pp 124–5(c) Courtesy of Alvin Boyarsky Archive

FROM ANOTHER PERSPECTIVE

A Word from *D* Editor
Neil Spiller

THE SAMIZDATS
Subversive Polemic

Samizdat: a system by which manuscripts denied official publication in the Soviet Union were circulated clandestinely in typescript or in mimeograph form, or were smuggled out for publication abroad.[1]

In what must have been the Autumn term of the 1992 academic year, my business partner and I were invited to attend an architectural review of student work at Vienna University of Technology (TU Wien) from a Coop Himmelb(l)au atelier/unit. The guest critic was Lebbeus Woods. This was the first time I had met him – the man whose 'Origins' show (1985), at the Architectural Association (AA) School of Architecture in London, had so captivated me and whose books were so enigmatic and graphically accomplished. On this occasion, we presented him with a copy of a small pamphlet, which we had self-published. It contained the drawings from our first 10 projects post architecture school – obviously all unbuilt. Lebbeus accepted the gift and, whilst flipping through it, an expression of palpable glee lit up his face. It was such a pleasure seeing his enjoyment!

It is with a similar glee that I now flip through the self–published booklets made by Lebbeus, that I and most of the architectural world never knew existed.

Before the Storm

Imagine the Earth not suffering with information overload as it does now, at a time where data was held at bay and electronic conduits did not hum with mundanities. There was no X/Twitter, Facebook, Instagram or TikTok; the phone was attached to the wall and one had to wait for the scheduled time to see a favourite television programme. The silence of the architectural profession was deafening and circumspect, with few architects putting their head above the parapet by expressing reservations about their field, its commercial dogmas and limited spatial palette. The profession had its eyes and ears mostly shut to the maverick, challenging ideas of upstart 'youths'.

How does one get one's subversive work out there? By self-publishing, of course, even if the results may be modest, due to the prohibitive cost of production.

Still, this method of self-publicity could work spectacularly well. A prime example is the group and zine Archigram, coined from an amalgamation of the words 'architecture' and 'telegram'. Active during the 1960s and early 1970s, the group produced polemic publications espousing the consumer and electronic possibilities for architecture in the age of the white heat of technology, the space race and the rapidly expanding potentials of communications.

During the latter 1970s, Lebbeus Woods produced a series of self-published works of his own, consisting of a mixture of polemic prose and fine, carefully drawn projects. It is unknown how many were printed or how they were distributed – giving them a somewhat mysterious status. Some carry an indication of the 'publisher', Augustän-Xenon Press.

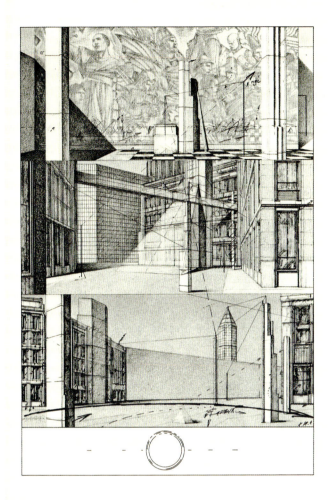

Lebbeus Woods,
Triptych,
1976

This vertical triptych combines two streetscapes and an interior; how they relate remains enigmatically unclear. Strong vertical elements that metamorphose and traverse the composite image provide a holistic compositional 'frame'.

Lebbeus Woods,
Cover of *HOUSE: Xn.,*
1979

opposite: Suspended between the grid and the rock, the theoretical house design evokes new ways to live and the new spatial arrangements such ways require. This version of the self-published volume's cover is hand-coloured by Woods.

As if to challenge the genre's intrinsic ephemerality, Woods's samizdats are neither cheap- nor spontaneous-looking at all. Printed on a fine creamy paper and carefully composed, all are arranged in portrait aspect ratio, and all are the same size (7.5 x 11 inches).

What is particularly interesting about their content is that they are at the cusp, showing a nascent architect at the point of finding his mature philosophical self and his unique visual lexicon. Seen together, the series is a catalytic outpouring of creativity with still-malleable ideas coagulating.

The first one (1976) is simply called *Triptych* and features one illustration – a vertical tripartite drawing – and no text. The architectural content and aspirations remain enigmatic whilst produced with a breathtaking graphic exactitude. The bottom panel of *Triptych* shows a ubiquitous American streetscape, including a blank wall. Seen peeking over the wall, in the middle distance, is what could be a commercial office tower or the external form of Woods's architecture. In the right-hand area in the foreground is what looks like a half-constructed square column; from its zenith radiate lines of connection to the select points of its surroundings. When one moves to the central panel, another streetscape is delineated – or perhaps the same, from another perspective? The top panel is an image of the interior – but can we be sure of that? What is more certain is that it has an almost ecclesiastical feel to it, with what might be an altar with a background of wall-painted heroic figures. Woods's trademark vectors and lines are there to be read but not understood.

Deconstructing the Domestic

Out of the nine samizdats, four describe projects for houses and villas – just drawings, no texts. The first, *HOUSE: J.* (1978), is the second publication in the series. On the front is a relatively traditional axonometric depiction, what one might describe as a De Stijl, slightly deconstructed building represented diagrammatically. The two pages inside are where the real graphic verve is. They contain an interior view and an external perspective. Again, vectors and lines choreograph both the internal space and the city air.

In 1979, the samizdats' production reached a rush of creativity. One finds two samizdats dedicated to extravagant villas, Villa Ä(--)X and Villae (U)R – situated on rocky outcrops, covered in abundant foliage, as if channelling Frank Lloyd Wright: Fallingwater (1935, Bear Run, Pennsylvania) or his earlier, more monolithic and defensive Los Angeles houses such as the Hollyhock House (1921) and Ennis House (1924). A call for the integration of arts is articulated in the volumes titled *Odysseus Wall Drawing*, *Architecture-Sculpture-Painting* and *Painting: Toward the Heroic*. Two other samizdats from this year include glimpses of the genesis of the 'AEON' project (1979–85), as well as HOUSE: Xn., a stylistic sibling to HOUSE: J..

Lebbeus Woods,
External perspective, *HOUSE: J.*,
1978

right: A work of great dexterity, HOUSE: J. has a more complex spatial configuration than the later HOUSE: Xn.. Its internal and external geometries are finely choreographed.

Lebbeus Woods,
Cover of *Odysseus Wall Drawing*,
1979

opposite: Here, 'the insatiable wanderer' receives a colour rendition.

130

Odysseus **Wall Drawing**

LEBBEUS WOODS   1979

'Our creative play in the continuous creation and recreation of living space is a dialogue with ourselves and each other, a catalyst of synthesis and civilization'

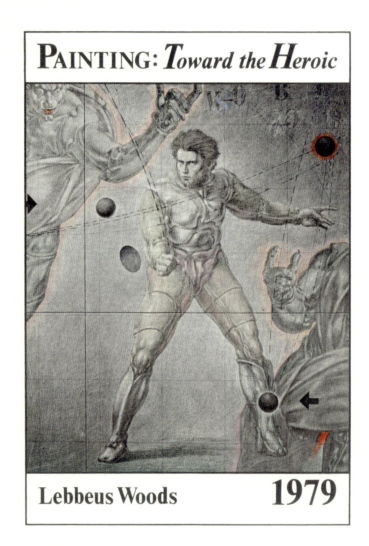

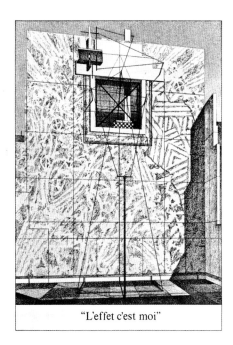

"L'effet c'est moi"

**Lebbeus Woods,
Drawing from *Architecture-Sculpture-Painting*,
1979**

above: A call for a synthesis of architecture, sculpture and painting: according to Woods, 'each an expression of some essential aspect of consciousness and experience'. The four drawings are interventions into an imagined city, with multi-scaled façades and patterned grids. Each proposition has a porosity in its elevational treatment, utilising and sometimes opening the grids.

**Lebbeus Woods,
Cover of *Painting: Toward the Heroic*,
1979**

opposite: In this samizdat, Woods rails against the false economics of the art market. What he articulated in 1979 is even more apposite and pronounced today. The cover is the only illustration; the content within is a polemic text.

In his writings from this period, Woods rallies against the world of exploitative dealers, aesthetically backward clients and the ongoing commodification of art/architecture treated as nothing more than an investment opportunity. Addressing the loss of architecture as a catalyst for change, social interaction and benevolent challenge, he argues for a new synthesis of painting, sculpture and architecture: 'The tensions existing between these arts are mirror-images of the tensions existing between our human faculties and experiences. Our creative play in the continuous creation and recreation of living space is a dialogue with ourselves and each other, a catalyst of synthesis and civilization.'[2]

'My Books Are My Buildings'
Sometime in 1993, I proffered a copy of the self-published booklet I'd given Lebbeus Woods to another hero at the Cooper Union in New York: John Hejduk, the Architecture School's iconic Dean, and a highly original producer of fantastic building designs and poetic prose. He, too, received my gift with great happiness, strode over to a metal cupboard in his office, opened it, and gave me a copy of every book he'd published by that time. As I was profusely thanking him, he simply said, 'My books are my buildings'. Many of us still know what he meant; others – born after the Storm – may yet find out.

It seems appropriate that a publication lit the fire of a wider appreciation of Woods's work. The *Origins* volume in the AA's 'Megas' series,[3] published to coincide with his exhibition of 1985, contributed to his international recognition. It also seems appropriate that the AA at the time was led by Alvin Boyarsky, an architectural impresario and the maker of many careers with his gift of love for exhibitions and books – the oxygen of fame.

One hopes that this 𝐷 will excite, inspire and intellectually invigorate, providing the points of entry into the early explorations of Lebbeus Woods, a kind man blessed with an extraordinary ability to draw and to speculate about what architecture might be. 𝐷

Notes
1. Collins online English dictionary, quoting *Webster's New World College Dictionary*, 4th edn: www.collinsdictionary.com/dictionary/english/samizdat.
2. Lebbeus Woods, *Architecture-Sculpture-Painting*, Augustän-Xenon Press (New York), 1979, p 3.
3. *Lebbeus Woods: Origins*, exhibition catalogue, AA Publications (London), 1985.

Text © 2024 John Wiley & Sons Ltd.
Images © The Estate of Lebbeus Woods

LEBBEUS WOODS:
EXQUISITE EXPERIMENTS, EARLY YEARS

Joseph Becker is the Associate Curator of Architecture and Design at the San Francisco Museum of Modern Art (SFMOMA), where his recent exhibitions include 'Marshall Brown Projects: Dequindre Civic Academy', 'Barbara Stauffacher Solomon: Strips of Stripes', 'Tauba Auerbach: S v Z' and 'Drawing the Line – Rael San Fratello at the US-Mexico Border'. His recent publications include *Tauba Auerbach – S v Z* (SFMOMA/DAP, 2020) and *The Sea Ranch: Architecture, Environment, and Idealism* (Prestel/DelMonico, 2018). In 2013, with Jennifer Dunlop Fletcher, he curated the retrospective exhibition 'Lebbeus Woods, Architect' at SFMOMA, the Broad Art Museum in Michigan and The Drawing Center, New York.

Aaron Betsky is a Professor in the School of Architecture and Design at Virginia Tech. He was previously Director of the school and, prior to that, President of the School of Architecture at Taliesin in Scottsdale, Arizona. Trained as an architect and in the humanities at Yale University, he has served as the Director of the Cincinnati Art Museum (2006–14) and the Netherlands Architecture Institute (2001–06), as well as Curator of Architecture and Design at SFMOMA (1995–2001). In 2008, he directed the 11th Venice Architecture Biennale. He writes the 'Beyond Buildings' twice-weekly blog for architectmagazine.com, and his latest books include *Fifty Lessons from Frank Lloyd Wright* (Rizzoli, 2021) and *Anarchitecture: The Monster Leviathan* (MIT Press, 2023).

Peter Cook was a founder of Archigram in the 1960s, taught at the Architectural Association (AA) in London from 1964 to 1990, and was a professor at the Städelschule, Frankfurt, from 1984 to 2009. He was Professor and Chair of the Bartlett School of Architecture, University College London (UCL) from 1990 to 2006, and is a RIBA Royal Gold Medalist (with Archigram). He has authored nine books, and his drawings are in the collections of the Museum of Modern Art (MoMA) in New York, Deutsches Architekturmuseum (DAM) in Frankfurt, Centre Pompidou in Paris and FRAC Centre in Orléans. His built works include the Kunsthaus Graz (2003) with Colin Fournier, and with his practice CRAB studio the departments of Law and Central Administration at the University of Vienna (2013), Abedian School of Architecture at Bond University, Gold Coast, Australia (2014) and the Drawing Studio at the Arts University Bournemouth (2016). He was knighted for services to architecture in 2007. During the pandemic he constructed the Innovation Studio with Tim Culverhouse, and has now joined new international practice CHAP (Cook, Haffner Architecture Platform) involved in projects in Asia, the Middle East and Norway.

Mark Dorrian holds the Forbes Chair in Architecture at the University of Edinburgh. He is Editor-in-Chief of *Drawing Matter Journal*, and a co-director of the practice Metis. His work spans topics in architecture and urbanism, art history and theory, and media studies. His books include *Writing on the Image: Architecture, the City and the Politics of Representation* (IB Tauris, 2015) and the co-edited volumes *Seeing From Above: The Aerial View in Visual Culture*, with Frédéric Pousin (IB Tauris, 2013) and *Drawing Architecture: Conversations on Contemporary Practice*, with Riet Eeckhout and Arnaud Hendrickx (Lund Humphries, 2022).

Riet Eeckhout is a guest professor and has a post-doctoral research position at the faculty of architecture of KU Leuven, Belgium. She exhibits, lectures and writes about the practice of research from within the discipline of architecture. Her drawings have been exhibited internationally, including at the Venice Architecture Biennale; La Gallerie d'Architecture, Paris; Tchoban Foundation – Museum of Architectural Drawing, Berlin; Architekturmuseum der TU Berlin; Art Omi: Architecture, New York; Design Centre UQAM, Montreal; and a83 gallery, New York City.

Kevin Erickson is an architect and principal of KNE studio based in New York City, and an Associate Professor at the University of Illinois at Urbana-Champaign where he has held positions of Program Chair and Director of Graduate Studies. He currently serves on the Radical Innovation Advisory Board. He was previously a member of the Van Alen Institute's Program Leadership Council, a visiting professor at the Mackintosh School of Architecture in Glasgow, and an artist-in-residence at the Geoffrey Bawa Lunuganga Trust in Sri Lanka.

Jörg H Gleiter is an architect and Professor of Architectural Theory at the Technical University Berlin. He was previously Professor of Aesthetics at Free University of Bolzano in Italy, and has held visiting professorships at Waseda University in Tokyo, Brown University in Providence, Rhode Island, the Bauhaus Universität Weimar, Politecnico di Torino and Politecnico di Milano. He is the founder of the book series *ArchitekturDenken* (Transcript Verlag Bielefeld). His books include *gleiters universum: architektur* (DEJAVU Gesellschaft, 2023); *Architekturtheorie zur*

CONTRIBUTORS

Einführung (Junius Verlag, 2022), *Ornament Today: Digital, Material, Structural* (Bozen-Bolzano University Press, 2012) and *Friedrich Nietzsche und die Architektur* (Königshausen & Neumann, 2009).

Sharon Irish is an architectural historian with particular interest in community cultural development and urban spatial practices. Most recently she published the monograph *Concerning Stephen Willats and the Social Function of Art: Experiments in Cybernetics and Society* (Bloomsbury, 2021). She has authored two other books and numerous articles. She holds a zero-time research affiliate appointment in the School of Information Sciences at the University of Illinois Urbana-Champaign.

Eliyahu Keller is an architect and architectural historian, currently serving as an assistant professor at the Faculty of Architecture and Town Planning at the Technion – Israel Institute of Technology in Haifa. He holds a PhD in History, Theory and Criticism of Architecture from the Massachusetts Institute of Technology (MIT), where he investigated the intersection of architectural representation, technological advancement, geopolitics and critical thinking. He is currently working on a manuscript exploring the influence of nuclear culture and apocalyptic thinking on speculative architectural imagination in the Cold War US.

Lawrence Rinder is Director Emeritus of the University of California, Berkeley Art Museum and Pacific Film Archive. He was Dean of the College at the California College of the Arts in San Francisco, and Founding Director of its Wattis Institute for Contemporary Arts. He was also previously Curator of Contemporary Art at the Whitney Museum of American Art in New York, where he organised exhibitions including the 2002 Whitney Biennial. He received a BA in art from Reed College in Portland, Oregon, and an MA in art history from Hunter College, New York City. He has taught art history at Columbia University, the University of California, Berkeley, and Deep Springs College, California.

Ashley Simone is an Associate Professor at the Pratt Institute School of Architecture in New York City, and Editorial Director of Applied Research + Design Publishing. She is the author of numerous essays on architecture and design, and editor of publications including *The Genealogy of Modern Architecture* (2015), *Absurd Thinking Between Art and Design* (2017), *Michael Webb: Two Journeys* (2018) and *In Search of African American Space* (2020), all published by Lars Müller.

Ben Sweeting teaches architecture and design at the University of Brighton. He encountered cybernetics through Neil Spiller and Ranulph Glanville while studying architecture at the Bartlett School of Architecture, University College London (UCL), going on to complete a PhD under their supervision that explored intersections between cybernetics and architectural design. His current work is situated between cybernetics, systemic design and architectural theory, with focuses on ethics, place, methodology and transdisciplinarity.

Lebbeus Woods was an American architect, architectural theorist and educator, whose home was the Irwin S Chanin School of Architecture at the Cooper Union, New York City. His work is represented in public and private collections including the San Francisco Museum of Modern Art (SFMOMA); Getty Research Institute, Los Angeles; Museum of Modern Art (MoMA), New York; MAK – Museum of Applied Arts, Vienna; Tchoban Foundation, Berlin; and M+, Hong Kong. Publications include *Einstein Tomb* (William Stout Publishers, 1980); *Origins* (AA Publications, 1985); *Terra Nova* (A+U, 1991); *ANARCHITECTURE: Architecture is a Political Act* (Academy Editions, 1992); *Earthquake!: A Post-Biblical View* (Springer, 2001); *System Wien* (Hatje Cantz, 2005); *Zagreb Free Zone Revisited* (University of Zagreb, 2021); and *OneFiveFour* (1989), *War and Architecture* (1993), *Radical Reconstruction* (1997), *The Storm and the Fall* (2004) and *Slow Manifesto: Lebbeus Woods Blog* (2015), all published by Princeton Architectural Press. Among other honours, Woods was a recipient of the Arts and Letters Award from the American Academy of Arts and Letters.

What is *Architectural Design*?

Founded in 1930, *Architectural Design* (△D) is an influential and prestigious publication. It combines the currency and topicality of a newsstand journal with the rigour and production qualities of a book. With an almost unrivalled reputation worldwide, it is consistently at the forefront of cultural thought and design.

Issues of △D are edited either by the journal Editor, Neil Spiller, or by an invited Guest-Editor. Renowned for being at the leading edge of design and new technologies, △D also covers themes as diverse as architectural history, the environment, interior design, landscape architecture and urban design.

Provocative and pioneering, △D inspires theoretical, creative and technological advances. It questions the outcome of technical innovations as well as the far-reaching social, cultural and environmental challenges that present themselves today.

For further information on △D and purchasing single issues see:

https://onlinelibrary.wiley.com/journal/15542769

Individual backlist issues of △D are available as books for purchase starting at £29.99 / US$45.00

wiley.com

Americas
E: cs-journals@wiley.com
T: +1 877 762 2974

Europe, Middle East and Africa
E: cs-journals@wiley.com
T: +44 (0)18 6577 8315

Asia Pacific
E: cs-journals@wiley.com
T: +65 6511 8000

Japan (for Japanese-speaking support)
E: cs-japan@wiley.com
T: +65 6511 8010

Visit our Online Customer Help
available in 7 languages at www.wileycustomerhelp.com/ask

Volume 93 No 2
ISBN 978-1-119-83835-7

Volume 93 No 3
ISBN 978-1-119-83442-7

Volume 93 No 4
ISBN 978-1-119-98396-5

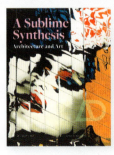

Volume 93 No 5
ISBN 978-1-394-17079-1

Volume 93 No 6
ISBN 978-1-394-16354-0

Volume 94 No 1
ISBN 978-1-394-17003-6